Hitting Below
the Bible Belt

Hitting Below the Bible Belt

Baptist Voodoo, Blood Kin, Grandma's Teeth and Other Stories from the South

Michael Chitwood

DOWN HOME

Down Home Press, Asheboro, N.C.

ISBN 1-878086-67-7

Library of Congress Catalog Card Number
98-071450

Printed in the United States of America

Book design by Beth Glover

Cover design by Tim Rickard

1 2 3 4 5 6 7 8 9

Down Home Press
P.O. Box 4126
Asheboro, N.C. 27204

To Carolyn and Jeffery, blood kin
and
For Lydia

Acknowledgments

Most of these essays were broadcast on WUNC, the public radio station in Chapel Hill, North Carolina. I would like to thank WUNC producer Paula Press for her suggestions and encouragement and the radio station for letting my accent get on the air. Also, I would like to thank the many listeners who let me know when one of these pieces rang especially true to them. To all of you: "No, you made *my* day."

"The Hunt Fund" was first published in *Voices from Home—The North Carolina Prose Anthology* published by Avisson Press.

"The Dangers of Hyphenation" won a creative non-fiction prize sponsored by the North Carolina Writers' Network.

Lines from C.D. Wright's poem "Our Dust" from her book *String Light* (University of Georgia Press, Athens) appear with permission of the author.

Lines from Robert Morgan's poem "When the Ambulance Came" from his book *Groundwork* (Gnomon Press, Frankfort, Kentucky) appear with permission of the author and press.

Foreword

"I grew up hunting, mostly rabbits," Michael Chitwood tells us. "There were rules...You didn't shoot a rabbit on the jump...You never shot in the direction of a person or dog." One of the most powerful passages in this extraordinary collection of essays describes how Chitwood's brother tracks a wounded deer to kill it: "I'm glad we found you," his brother said, field-dressing the animal on the spot. "He was up to his elbows inside the deer. "'I would have felt terrible if we hadn't found you.'"

But this intimate connection with the natural world, the world of Chitwood's childhood and youth in the mountains of Virginia, has been broken. Now he teaches at the University of North Carolina—wears a sports jacket, has an office. Until recently he "worked in the Research Triangle Park, North Carolina...About 34,000 people come to work each day in the Park...We all work in offices or laboratories—eight, ten, twelve hours inside each day." The company he worked for was researching virtual reality. "Eventually you will be able to drive through a town, walk through a house or rearrange the furniture in a room without moving from in front of the computer monitor." By contrast, Chitwood's brother, a construction company owner, still hunts with their father "the entire opening week of deer season." This brother lives "four miles from my parents on land purchased with money my parents gave him, the equivalent of the sum required for my college education. Which is more real," Chitwood asks us, "an idea or an acre?"

It's a question he will ponder throughout this entire collection, a question which reflects the Southerner's classic preoccupations with place, with the past, with family and home. Who are we when we don't (can't) live there any more? What can we keep from the past? What should we jettison? Can anything ever take the place of what we must inevitably lose? Though he's no longer that mountain boy with a gun—flanked by family, at home in the woods—Michael Chitwood is still hunting for the answers to these questions.

Those early years brought gifts which have endured. His grandmother was closely linked to the land, the seasons, and especially the moon. "It told her when to plant potatoes, when to can peaches, when it would snow." Though he declares it's "time to move on. Time to download the calico and get over the old-fashioned grandmotherly notion that we are a people connected to the landscape"—it's clear that he will not, cannot do so. Because of her, he will always notice the moon, "a huge open letter from her to me." The essays describing her decline and death are among the toughest and most beautiful in this book.

Like the hunting piece, the essays on tobacco make us uneasy, raise questions. Isn't hunting wrong? Doesn't tobacco kill us? Sure, but there's a romance to it, too, which Chitwood explains in "Tobacco People" and "Green Like Money." Though his grandfather, an inveterate Lucky Strike smoker died, "gasping for breath," at sixty-one, Chitwood can still recall the thrill of walking home at the end of the first week of priming tobacco at age fourteen, clutching three twenty-dollar bills. "And every step sounded like *rich, rich, rich.*" We learn how racism was played out in a dark Methodist Church basement, where a troop of Scouts played a questionable game called "Ships in the Fog." "In that innocent dark, you couldn't tell what color the lip was that your elbow split. You couldn't see the shade of the forehead that bruised your cheek. All blood was equal on the hard tile of the Methodist basement floor. Down there in God's cellar, Ships in the Fog, we exchanged our rough shoulder-cracking hugs and earned our Citizenship badges."

Chitwood's refusal to settle for easy answers extends to present-day life as well. Parenting is both wonderful and terrible—every parent will identify with his description of "the five to seven o'clock gauntlet." In "The Three A.M. Stare," possibly the best piece in the book, he reminds us that "there's nothing innocent about a newborn's steely stare" that asks "What are you to me?" or "Will you be able to love me enough; will I you?"

Though Chitwood won't accept the consolations of the quick fix, the simplistic solution, he continues to search. Why? What's he looking for? Hard for even a poet to say, but he edges up on it as he describes the "elegiac feeling" of early spring. "Rather than the elation of new birth, I feel a wistfulness, a kind of unfocused longing. It's the feeling of trying to recall something you should have written down, had intended to write down, but you didn't and now, though you know it was something important, you can't summon it." He comes even closer as he writes about that "certain slant of light/winter afternoons" as Emily Dickinson called it. "Light is not metaphorical and our journey in it is not allegorical," he tells us. "It's real and dangerous and we must pay careful attention and sometimes even that won't be enough." Perhaps not, but it's all we can do, isn't it, those among us with a poet's soul and a hunter's keen eye? Personally, I'm glad Michael Chitwood is still out there in the woods, still hunting and taking note.

Lee Smith
Hillsborough, N.C., April 1998

Contents

That's What I Like about the South

Green like Money

I loved my grandfather's ashtray. It sat beside his rocking chair on a pedestal, just at arm rest level. Every Saturday afternoon he and I would settle in for "Wrestling from Roanoke"—Wahoo McDaniel, Swede Hanson, Blackjack Mulligan and Johnny Weaver. He would unzip the chest pocket of his bibs and fish for his pack of Lucky Strikes.

While the boys on TV body-slammed each other and then raged about retribution next week, thin ribbons of smoke drifted from the ashtray. Toward the end of the hour, he would say, "Alright." That's all, just the one word signal. I would hurry over to his chair and put both thumbs on the brown button at the edge of the ashtray.

It seemed to take my full weight to press the button and make the twin trap doors fly open and drop an hour's worth of ashes into darkness.

The ashtray fired my imagination. Those trap doors snapped down, and knights, explorers, treasure hunters fell to dungeons. And then, the afternoon's real hero would say, "Why don't we ride out to Moran's and get a cold drink."

He died, gasping for breath, at age sixty-one.

Michael Chitwood

Even before the red light of the ambulance could run through the yard, he was dead in my father's arms—massive heart attack is the way my father always describes it.

I'm sure those Lucky Strikes helped kill him. I'm sure that every Saturday afternoon he was sipping his own death through those short white straws. I'm just as sure that he wouldn't have quit smoking, even knowing the health risks. Tobacco was as much a part of him as his bibs and pocket watch. He'd raised it most of his life. Tobacco meant new shoes, new cars, a paid tab at Moran's.

Just about everybody I knew growing up in Southwest Virginia raised or had just recently stopped raising tobacco. I'd seen many adults pull in a long whiff of the aroma coming from a tobacco barn and say, "Smells like money." For many rural Southerners, that's exactly what it is—the only crop they can raise with the major investment being just their time and long effort.

I'm not a smoking advocate; I know there's a trap door ready to fall out from under every smoker. But I also know the lure of tobacco money in communities that don't have entrance ramps to the information super highway.

At the end of my first week of priming tobacco— the hardest, dirtiest work I've ever done—I was handed three twenty-dollar bills. I was fourteen. It was the most money I'd ever held. All the way home, I scuffed my Converses in the gravel of the road, too tired to take a normal step. And every step sounded like *rich, rich, rich.*

Rough Weather

I'd stopped for coffee and the guy in front of me at the fast food counter was chatting—no, he was tormenting the young woman taking his money.

"I thought you guys would be closing. Doesn't everything down here close when the first icicle forms?" (I think this is what passes for polite conversation in New Jersey.)

The woman behind the counter didn't rise to his taunt; she just smiled and handed him his order. I said nothing but spent the rest of my trip trying to stay alert for ice patches and thinking about what the guy had said.

I now feel honor bound to give a brief explanation of the Southern approach to driving in inclement weather.

Okay, I'll admit that schools and businesses here do tend to bolt the doors at the first sign of rough weather. I could offer an excuse such as the highway department doesn't have the equipment to handle serious ice and snow. Why should they? With most of our "snows" you can't make a decent snow elf. But lack of equipment isn't the real reason a flake of snow can clear a building here faster than a fire drill.

The real reason is that even the threat of snow creates for every Southerner a kind of impromptu Mardi Gras. We spend the bulk of the year sweating or dashing from air conditioned cars into air conditioned houses. Most of the time, asphalt here can blister your soles if your shoes are too worn. Snow is like falling aspirin, easing the hot hurt of the whole landscape.

The party-time atmosphere addresses another complaint non-Southerners have about Dixie-born drivers. It's not, as some allege, that we *can't* drive in the snow. I've seen my mother, determined to get to some destination or other, take a 1965 Country Sedan station wagon through two-foot drifts. During a storm, folks in the Southern mountains will throw ten or twelve cinder blocks in the back of the pickup and not only get their mommas to church but take them visiting afterwards. The truth of the matter is we don't *want* to plod along in the traffic ruts. There are few greater thrills than getting a couple tons of steel spinning like a Tilt-A-Whirl on a semi-deserted two-lane.

See we're just out having fun. The explanation's that simple. But here's something I can't explain: I've noticed that no matter how many non-Southerners a building may contain there's no reduction in the building clearing time. Not once have I heard a transplanted Vermonter come out of her office and exclaim, "The rest of you go on and buy out all the milk in the state. I'll stay here and catch the phones." In fact, I heard one guy from Maine do a passable rebel yell when the head-for-home signal was given.

Baptist Voodoo

I blame it on New Orleans, the jazz-haunted land of dreamy dreams. I mean what else could account for those perfectly reasonable Southern Baptists seeming to go...well...wacko. I think someone worked a mojo hand on them or got some High John the Conqueror root for a hex.

Look at the evidence. The Southern Baptist convention, which in 1996 in the Crescent City, has in the past taken such thoughtful, forward-looking stances on issues. Think about how quickly they embraced their brethren black Baptists and spoke out against racism in every form. Why, as early as 1995, they issued an apology for any prejudicial actions or inactions they may have inadvertently perpetrated. And I learned at my Baptist grandmother's knee the reasonable, hard-shell position on women in the pulpit and the healthful effects of vigorous dancing.

So it must have been some kind of hoodoo. Again, look at the evidence. The convention announces a boycott of the Walt Disney corporation—its theme parks and products including movies. The Disney

Michael Chitwood

corporation must suffer this crippling blow because it has granted, along with numerous other companies including major pharmaceutical producers, benefits to the domestic partners of its employees, which would include gay and lesbian partners. The convention did not encourage its members to stop taking their heart or ulcer medications.

Then a spokesman for the convention admits on national radio that he plans to continue using his family passes to Disneyland because he had already bought those and Disney had the money. Only a beyond-the-grave spell from Marie Laveau herself could work that kind of wackiness.

And then, after they got through with The Devil Mouse and his empire, they announced a major program to convert Jews from their millenniums of belief.

I'm telling you it's disturbing. I mean people might start making fun of the Baptists and forget their history of tolerance and brotherly love. Oh why, oh why couldn't they have gone to Des Moines or Davenport?

I tell you this kind of thing could get out of hand. Right now, I'm getting this incredible desire to watch *101 Damnations*...I mean *Dalmatians*. Quick, somebody pass me a copperhead, I've got to expel this demon.

Music in a Dark House

Hurricane Fran's darkness deepened for me on the Monday after the storm when I learned that the father of Bluegrass music, Bill Monroe, had died. Here, I was in a house without electricity or water, unable to listen in tribute to my favorite Monroe tunes.

I grew up on Bluegrass. But let me admit publicly that I grew up on it reluctantly. Every morning of my youth, as my brother, sister and I got ready for school and Mom and Dad dressed for work, WYTI broadcast from the beige Zenith radio on the counter. Known throughout the county (and without irony I have to add) as "Whitey" radio, the station played country and bluegrass. They aren't the same thing by the way. Bluegrass is entirely acoustic—usually a mandolin (Monroe's instrument), a fiddle, banjo, guitar and bass, maybe a dobro, too. "Foggy Mountain Breakdown," which most folks know as the theme of *Bonnie and Clyde*, "The Ballad of Jed Clampett" and "Duelin Banjos" (the theme of *Deliverance*) are the popular incarnations of Bluegrass.

Anyway, Whitey played it and I complained about wanting to hear rock and roll. If fact, I hated that twangy stuff, I said. But I was also, subconsciously, listening. I was listening at the bloodstream level, which is where Bluegrass works best. This string music is to popular music what poetry is to modern literature. Which is to say, the red-headed stepchild, to use a mountain phrase. But these neglected forms preserve the wild essence of their more celebrated and sanitized cousins.

Somewhere about 1974, I discovered that Bluegrass had infected me. Fiddler's conventions were springing up in every good-sized cow pasture, and smoking local bands were looking to join Lester and Earl (who were early members of Monroe's band) on the television.

I keep an image from those weekend-long music parties always at the ready—people would carry around small squares of plyboard that, when the music raged, they would throw down and dance on, amid thistles, cow pies and mud. Totin your own dance floor. Now that's joy. That's powerful music.

So on that Monday, I did a few steps in a dark house. Fitting, I guess, since this Appalachian music was often made in rooms without electricity or running water. I hummed some "Uncle Pen" and "Blue Moon of Kentucky." And I said out loud to the folks on the other side of Jordan, "Y'all get your plyboard ready. Daddy Bill's on the way."

The Battleground

Northern Ireland. The former Yugoslavia. Chechnya. I've had trouble understanding these long-standing tribal hatreds. Often I've lobbed questions over my newspaper—"What's wrong with these people? That stuff happened decades ago. Can't they see what this brutal feuding is doing to their country, to their future?" Common sense comes easily when you're in your favorite chair, enjoying your morning coffee.

Of course, there's no one more obnoxious than a person at peace with his untested beliefs. And no one more ready for a takedown. Naturally, I didn't see it coming.

My college friends and I, headed for a canoeing adventure in Canada, had decided to break up the trip with a stop at Gettysburg. We'd all read Michael Shaara's stunning book *The Killer Angels*, which recounts the famous bloodletting, and thought we'd stretch our legs on Lincoln's "hallowed ground."

We took in the whole battlefield from the tower erected for that purpose and had a gentlemen who was waiting for his tour group to collect take our picture with the scene of Pickett's ill-fated charge in the background. Then we decided to drive over to the North Carolina and Virginia memorials, since we had strong ties to both states.

The license plates along the road behind the memorials were predictable, although I hadn't thought of it before—Georgia, the Carolinas, Tennessee, Virginia. Everyone spoke quietly, pointing out landmarks to companions, walking a little ways out into the field and then just standing and looking into the August haze. The feeling at the Virginia memorial, where George Pickett's division lined up to start their march into slaughter, was absolutely reverent.

We hardly spoke as we rode over to Little Round Top, the rise from which the federal guns pounded the Southerners. I couldn't help but notice the change in license plates—Pennsylvania, New York, Vermont. Children scampered over the rocks; parents called to them. A man clapped another's back after the punch line of a joke. It was like a Fourth of July picnic.

"Easy to see who was doing the killing and who was doing the dying," I hissed to one of my friends.

"Let's get out of here," he said, already turning back toward the car.

I was surprised by the anger that had come so quickly to both our voices. One hundred and thirty-three years and these fields are still haunted, I thought. But now, recollecting it, I know it wasn't those green fields that were cursed. The ghosts reside in the hot, panicky, tribal lodge of the human skull.

God help us.

Notes from the Dead

The first tree I could climb was the little dogwood in our backyard. Barely more than a shrub, the tree forked about three feet from the ground and had several limbs that were easy to reach. When I had conquered the topmost branches, I was, oh, every bit of six feet off the ground.

The first tree you can climb likely is also the first tree you fall out of, and that was the case with the little dogwood. Actually I didn't make it all the way out of the tree, just back down to the fork where the broken remnant of a limb stopped my fall by implanting itself in my lower leg. I had received my first scar.

A little later I would hear during an Easter service the legend of the dogwood, how it once grew to lofty heights, and because of its strength was the tree used to make the cross on which Jesus was crucified. For that assistance in man's salvation (I never understood this part, although it's the linchpin of the message), God cursed the tree, condemning it to be stunted and frail, staining its blossom with red at the tips of the four white petals.

Maybe it's the scar and the mystifying curse that

Michael Chitwood

have given me a lifelong fascination with the little tree. I get an elegiac feeling in the early Spring when the redbuds bloom and I know the dogwoods won't be far behind. Rather than the elation of new birth, I feel a wistfulness, a kind of unfocused longing. It's the feeling of being unable to recall something that you should have written down, had intended to write down, but didn't, and now, though you know it was something important, you can't summon it.

Though I still can't really articulate the feeling, I read something about two years ago that resonated with it and has become for me a parallel image, an emotional twin.

Toward the end of the Civil War, Southern foot soldiers going into battle knew it was very likely that they would not survive. They wrote their names and hometowns on small pieces of paper and pinned them inside a coat or shirt in hopes that at least their bodies would be returned to loved ones. For the most part, these were men of strong Christian heritage, so they must have believed their souls would be elsewhere and otherwise occupied after the battle. It was a last minute thought for the body, an ultimate form of homesickness.

Now when I see those dogwood blossoms, particularly on a moonlit evening when they are luminous, I think of those notes and the longed-for destinations of the senses. The soul, or any eternal spirit, can't ache at the sight of those papery, brief notions. You need an ever perishing body for that.

Ships In The Fog

Troop 362 met in the basement of the Methodist Church. Maybe that explains it. Maybe there in God's cellar, or Hell's attic, we felt some higher moral calling.

Anyway, we promised to be trustworthy, loyal, helpful, friendly, courteous, kind, obedient, cheerful, thrifty, brave, clean, reverent, and, we always amended, hungry. We practiced our knots. We had our patrol meetings. We bent to place the life-saving kiss on Resusci-Annie and laughed in the embarrassment of saving a doll. Was this what making out was like? The taste of plastic and a swirl in the pit of your stomach?

After all the business was taken care of, we played Ships in the Fog. A scoutmaster would be hauled into court these days for allowing such a game, but those were more innocent times, and, as I've said, we were in the basement of the church. What harm could we do?

The room was cleared of tables and chairs and two chalk circles were drawn at opposite ends. The boys were divided into two groups and corralled into the circles. There were no windows in the basement room, just concrete walls and a hard tiled floor. When the lights went out the place was dark as a grave.

The object of the game was to exchange circles in the dark. Anyone outside a circle when the lights came back on had to stand in the hallway with the leader and his assistant. If you could drag someone from the opposing circle with you into yours, they also had to quit the game.

Like I said, it was the basement of the church, and we were scouts. So none of the boys said anything when Chuck Edwards joined the troop. This was a rural troop in the early 1970s. The reforms that were sweeping the nation were just arriving in this community. We heard our parents whispering that Chuck was a plant, a test by the NAACP to see what we would do. I felt the old swirl in my stomach. Chuck was a nice guy, small and quick. He tied some of our best knots.

To our credit, and our parents' credit, we did nothing. We practiced our craft and recited our oath. And when the scoutmaster doused the light, we charged. In that innocent dark, you couldn't tell what color the lip was that your elbow split. You couldn't see the shade of the forehead that bruised your cheek. All blood was equal on the hard tile of the Methodist basement floor. Down there, in God's cellar, Ships in the Fog, we exchanged our rough, shoulder-cracking hugs and earned our citizenship badges.

The Graduation

It's June, 1976, the successful tobacco about knee-high. Rodney, Tony and I have just graduated from high school. Our lives have begun, we say to each other, though I don't know what we had lived up to that point if not our lives.

Rodney has borrowed his parents' Dodge. At least, I think it was a Dodge. It was a new model anyway with the latest Detroit invention, push-button gears on the dashboard. You just "selected" your gear as you drove along, everything at your fingertips.

This was a great source of embarrassment to Rodney, who certainly did not want to "select" a gear. A junior Junior Johnson, Rodney wanted to double clutch, speed shift and get rubber. He didn't want his friends to see him push a button for second gear. Maybe that was why he was doing what he was doing. Or maybe it was because our lives had begun.

We had scored some beer at a remote convenience store and had already stopped to write our initials, with urine, in the dust of a dead-end gravel road.

Michael Chitwood

We were cruising the state routes and washboard county roads, the ones barely wide enough for a single car. Rodney had decided to floor it. Gravels were pinging the undercarriage and dust billowed in our wake. As we approached an intersection with a paved road, Rodney began screaming and whooping, sticking his head out the window.

Just as we hit the asphalt, he cut the wheel hard and started the car in a tight circle. I heard gravel again, then pavement, then gravel and Rodney screaming. Four, five times we went around, spraying the young tobacco leaves in the roadside field with a cloud of dust.

So what were we graduating from that night? From nothing and into our lives? Or from our lives and into nothing? Why was it so quickening to be cutting donuts for an audience of future cigarettes? Why did we have the family sedan, which would be sitting piously in the church parking lot the next morning, spinning?

The scary truth of it is I don't know. I didn't then and I don't now. I can only say that I was able to watch the plume of our spinning drift off to powder the young plants and finally settle back to the field, dust to dust. For that, I'm grateful.

The Handkerchief of the Lord

It begins to happen in March. At the office around the coffee pot. At soccer practice. In the parking lot after church. Men, in conspiratorial knots, nodding solemnly, making small reverent gestures.

From the look of the group, you might think they were discussing the death of an eminent citizen or some weighty political matter. But do you know what they're really talking about? It's grass. No, not the mind-altering substance from the hemp plant. The stuff in their yards—or at least the stuff they hope will soon be in their yards.

If you could measure importance by the amount of space a particular subject occupies in conversation, then "The Yard" or "The Lawn" is surely a sacred concern of men, especially Southern men. From early spring until the last mowing in the fall, for many men, the grass will be a flag of disposition, out of hopeful green stuff woven, to paraphrase the good, gray poet.

It sounds silly, but it's serious, a lesson I learned during the summer of 1978 when I was inducted into the brotherhood of the yard, very much against my

Michael Chitwood

will. I was between my sophomore and junior years in college and earning my next year's spending money by working in a textile mill.

My ride—the family couldn't spare me a car—was one of the weavers, and every afternoon he would settle on a wooden bench outside the weave room to discuss yard lore with some of the other workers. They rated the qualities of Kentucky 31 and Falcon fescue. They advised about when Shady Knock or Creeping Red was called for. They suggested curatives for brown patches and hard-packed soil. I stood out in the sunny parking lot, burning to go. I was as silent as the grass they revered, hoping my ride would take the hint. I had things to do. I had a life to get on with.

All summer I fumed and chafed at the repetitive lines of their conversation that kept me tied to that parking lot. But that fall, in American Studies, I came upon these lines: "I guess it is the handkerchief of the Lord,/ A scented gift and remembrancer designedly dropped..../ I guess it is a uniform hieroglyphic..../ And now it seems to me the beautiful uncut hair of graves."

All that summer Walt Whitman had sat with the weaver, the cloth doffer, the fixer. He had murmured with them. He knew that what they had to say wasn't necessarily as important as just their saying it. That even though the shade crept over them, they sat and did not hurry. With dirt under their fingernails and grease on their shirts, they translated the green hieroglyphic. They read me its slow message.

"They are alive and well somewhere,/ The smallest sprout shows there is really no death,/ And if ever there was it led torward life, and does not wait at the end to arrest it,/ And ceased the moment life appeared."

The Helicopter

I was about eight when Harvey, our neighbor, decided to build the helicopter.

Harvey had seven years of formal education. He planted his potatoes and beans by the signs. He believed the government, federal, state or county, should not stick its nose in your business. He believed man had dominion over the beasts of the field and the birds of the air. We knew he would build the helicopter.

Harvey's workshop, a garage with double wooden doors, was slightly larger than his house. That seemed proper since he spent more time in the workshop anyway. Some of the local engineers, men with full high school educations, began to tease Harvey, asking him about his jet.

"It's a helicopter," Harvey would answer. "Y'all just watch."

Harvey worked inside the workshop at first, tuning and re-tuning a big Cummins engine. It might have been a White, the engineers couldn't agree on that. But when it was time to put the helicopter together, Harvey had to move his operation into view of all the curious.

He pieced together the frame from the surplus of a greenhouse skeleton. The rotor blades were some kind of blond wood that Harvey, after getting them into place, decided were too heavy so he took them off and hollowed them out. He would control the bird from an old school bus seat bolted to two-by-fours.

The day finally came, and Harvey allowed a crowd to gather before he started the engine. Some of the engineers shouted for Harvey to be sure and write from wherever he landed. Harvey revved the engine to drown them out. Inside the cage of greenhouse pipe, he looked like a scrawny bird perched nervously on a bus seat.

He began working throttles, and the blades whirled, then disappeared with speed. To whoops and squeals, the helicopter began to bounce around the yard. Harvey worked frantically inside the cage. The crowd dispersed in every direction.

The helicopter moved around the yard like a panicked chicken, half flying and half running, and Harvey had the look of a man who didn't know if it would be smarter to hold on or let go.

Finally, he managed to calm the bucking machine. He shut down the engine and got out, trying to calmly check gauges, but he kept one hand on the frame for support. "Just needs a little fine tuning," he announced to the engineers who gathered around to seriously study this invention.

Harvey said the call came the following Monday. "FAA boys out of Roanoke. Said I didn't have a certified craft or pilot's license."

The helicopter sits on the hill behind the workshop now. Harvey likes for people to ask about it. "Ah, damn government," he'll say. "I'd love to fly it. I'd fly it tomorrow, if they would let me."

Southern Exposure

Okay, I'll admit that at first it made me mad. I steamed up in the short walk from the mail box to the house. The cover of *The New Yorker* sported the Olympic rings, waving crowds and a rotund hayseed, complete with straw hat, bib overalls, smiling pig tucked under one arm and a sash reading, "Howdy."

Howdy? I slammed the magazine on the kitchen table and was working up a good rant about ignorant Yankee cartoonists when it hit me. This was perfect. This was just perfect. I, we, all of us, the whole cotton-choppin, 'bacca priming, banjo pickin' South had them right where we wanted them. We, true native-born Southerners, are completely camouflaged. When New York, or L.A., or wherever looks to the lower right corner of the country, they see the MGM facade we've prepared for them, which means, of course, that we can have our way with them.

"Not true," I hear top-hatted Eustace Tilly shout from Park Avenue. "We know about you dirt-eating, cousin-loving crackers." And we answer, "Sho nuf, bubba. You got us pegged like a pit-bull next to a doublewide. Bring some of that Wall Street funny money down here, and we'll show you great big ol' alligators."

Think I'm making this up? Consider this then. An old college buddy of mine (us graduates of LSU, UVa, Georgia, Carolina and Sewanee are big on old college buddies) spent his summers working at the Williamsburg Pottery. He would often tell us how the pottery's owner chuckled as he strode through the parking lot full of license plates from New Jersey, Pennsylvania and Maine. "You can sell to the classes and eat with the masses or sell to the masses and eat with the classes," the owner would muse. Williamsburg Pottery, South of the Border, Gatlinburg. Enough said.

And what better example of camouflage could there be than Pretty Miss Dolly Parton, as she was known on "The Porter Wagoner Show"? The innocent little mountain girl with the platinum hair and silicon-fortified prow crooks her finger and says "Y'all come on down to Dollywood, ya hear." Dolly has also said, publicly, that she laughs all the way to the bank. And, when we hear her sing "Rosewood Casket" or "Farther Along," we know that the soul of the lady from Pigeon Forge is still intact and in touch with those Tennessee Smokies.

So, Mr. New York cartoonist, keep drawing. Hey, you left out the moonshine jug. And what? No copperheads?

Tobacco People

I've been thinking a lot about the Thurmans lately. The county road that ran by my childhood home dead-ended at the Thurman farm. The school bus would lumber into the too-small turning circle in front of the Thurmans' six-room house and have to back up and pull forward several times to get turned around. Then Kay and the three Thurman boys would get on the bus.

The smallest Thurman, John Moses, four years my junior, seemed large to me. He already had visible muscles in his arms. When I was old enough for my first job besides mowing Grandma's yard, I would find out why John Moses had muscles. He, and all the Thurmans, worked. I don't mean feeding the dog or setting the table for an allowance. They were tobacco farmers, which as everyone in our county knew, was a thirteen-month-a-year job.

The Thurmans, I would discover in the summer I worked for them, were a rural cliché. Billy, the oldest boy, supervised the tobacco priming until Papa got home from his public works job—that's what they called it, anything off the farm was public works. Billy,

39

Michael Chitwood

Danny, John Moses and I primed all day. Kay and Mrs. Thurman cooked and took care of barn chores such as feeding the calves, for the Thurmans also raised cattle for beef. Cooking was a major chore because after working all morning in the tobacco fields, Billy, Danny and John Moses ate like the front line of the Washington Redskins. We would go through two loaves of bread at each meal. They would argue over who got the last spoonful of beans.

The other part of the Thurmans' rural stereotype was the way they lived. They seemed, to me, to be packed into a simple house. They were in church every Sunday. They did not drink. And they did not smoke. Almost every day, Billy would hold out his hands, after we had been priming for several hours, and say, "This is what smoking does to you lungs." Our hands would be black with the sticky tar-like resin of the plants.

While not a single Thurman used the "cancer sticks," the "coffin nails," they raised acres and acres of the plant. They made a sizable income each year from the sale of what they knew to be a toxin. And I made what seemed like a fortune at the time from helping them.

"If people want to smoke it, we'll raise it," Billy would say, his arms bulging as he unloaded a rack from the primer. My goal for the summer was to have the veins in my arms pop out like Billy's did.

Now, when I hear of the latest victory for "Big Tobacco" in a wrongful death case, or of another state queuing up to get in on the lawsuits against the tobacco giants, I think of the robust Thurmans and the land they bought with the profits. I think of all the Thurman-like families across the South. And, thinking of them, I don't know what to think.

Church and State

Snakes • The Politics of Religion • The Red Words • The Dangers of Hyphenation • The Voices of the People • A Poem for the Nation • The Unspoiled Past • Bread and Circuses • Whispers • Y • Questions • Old Virginny

Snakes

There's nothing like an unexpected encounter with a snake to restore one's religious beliefs. I've heard hard-cussing, beer-bellied construction workers call on Jesus Christ and the Lord God Almighty in one snatch of breath, just because an unearthed black snake has rolled from a backhoe bucket and draped himself around their shoulders.

I love the effect snakes have on most people. Leave a harmless corn snake on either of my grandmothers' living room couches, and those women would achieve ecstasies to make Saint Teresa proud. I'm convinced that an abundancy of serpents is the reason the South is so deeply religious; the Bible Belt has a distinctive diamond-backed pattern.

That's going to be the ultimate downfall of the Jerry Falwells and Pat Roberstons, and their puppets like Oliver North. To transform themselves into politicians, the electronic evangelists are shedding their biblical skins for dark suits and Limbaugh lies. But hearing spook tales about bogeymen just doesn't do the same thing to your bowels as coming eye-to-eye with a real cottonmouth.

Michael Chitwood

The trouble for most people is it's been a while since they had an encounter of the legless reptilian kind. That's why the two-legged variety thrives; they provide the venom that gets people's adrenaline pumping.

For instance, several members of my family and I were on my grandmother's front porch, embroiled in a rant about evangelists turning into politicians. We were so caught up in our discussion that we didn't notice, at least for awhile, that a five-foot black snake had joined our little party. When my sister suddenly stopped breathing, jerked my young son from his play on the floor and, tucking the boy under her arm like a football, left the porch in a dead run, I noticed our visitor.

The porch cleared rapidly. Once inside, my grandmother began screaming out the window for me to kill the snake. She would not sleep, ever again, she warned if I didn't chop its head off. And, I had to do it where she could see it die.

I didn't want her up until all hours, maybe turning to Rush in desperation, so I hacked the snake with a hoe. Then I noticed a large bulge in its mid-section. My father and I decided to see what the snake's last meal had been. My father's pocketknife unzipped the poor serpent and out rolled a squirrel-sized rat.

It smacked the ground and woke, screamed, defecated and bolted for cover. We looked at each other stunned. At the time, we didn't know what to make of it. But I've come to understand. It's a sign. That's what it really means to be born again.

The Politics of Religion

It's like a mental snapshot, the moment gone in a flash, but its artifact always in my memory.

My father and I are nose-to-nose, in one of the many pitched battles of my adolescence. We're discussing politics, if you consider his lecturing and my sarcastic, bitten-off retorts as discussing. I'm regurgitating the ideas of my devil's advocate government teacher and he's toeing the company line his plant manager has shown him.

"Honest people don't need handouts," he growls. "They're willing to work."

"Is that what your Christianity teaches you?" I say. At that point in life I was willing to use anything to win an argument. But I instantly knew I'd gone too far. He got too calm, too quiet.

Almost in a whisper, he said, "You can make fun of my politics, but don't you make fun of my religion." There was both pain and real anger in his eyes. My mother, sensing that things could shortly get out of hand, said, "Alright, that's enough."

My father and mother are life-long Christians. My mother's fond of saying she was rocked in a Methodist cradle. Ever since I can remember, my Dad has gone to choir practice on Wednesday night, and the whole family was in church on Sunday morning. If there was a spaghetti supper, ice cream supper, Brunswick stew making or sausage-and-egg breakfast to raise money for the church, my folks were some of the first to arrive and last to leave.

They believe way down deep. But they don't make a show of it except in the way they live. They don't hide their light under a bushel, but they don't hold you down and interrogate you with it either.

That's probably why I'm so nervous about the recent movements to give religion and politics a church wedding. It's dangerous ground, because if you disagree with someone's politics, you're passing judgment on their religion. That's serious business in a country founded by people looking for religious freedom. Thomas Jefferson considered his Statute of Virginia for Religious Freedom one of his greatest accomplishments and prescribed that it be listed with two others on his tombstone. That he was President of the United States was not on the list.

People should vote, or for that matter, do anything according to their moral code. What's worrisome is that the folks who are reading the vows at the marriage of religion and politics are performers. They make a television show of their religion. They use it to get votes. It's scary. I just hope that when the "discussion" they're getting started is about to become a fistfight, there's somebody around to say, "Alright, that's enough."

The Red Words

We sang about Zacchaeus coming down from the tree. We clipped figures from the Big Book of Bible Heroes and pasted them onto colored construction paper with some tasty glue concoction. We played Red Rover. We went home around lunch time with our tongues bright red from the Kool-Aid. And, at the end of that week of Vacation Bible School, we got a special treat—a deluxe edition New Testament.

I didn't really look at my Bible until I got home. I was about to toss it onto my dresser but decided to crack it open for some reason. On almost every page, it seemed the book had broken out in welts. Sometimes it was just a sentence or two. Sometimes nearly the whole page had turned red, like a rash, like the book was catching fire.

I dropped the book. "Mom, something's wrong with the Bible," I screamed.

Well, of course, I had just been awarded a Bible in which all the words attributed to Jesus were printed in red. It was probably some Christian marketer's brainstorm and had resulted in millions of sales for the publishing company. But it was a spooky moment for a kid thinking about getting to the swimming pool.

That Bible floated back into my mind recently when I read some comments televangelist Pat Robertson made to an audience of the faithful. After he invited any reporters who might be in the room to shoot themselves, Robertson announced that his Christian Coalition was a "seasoned group of warriors" who would determine who the next president of the United States would be.

Robertson also had some names to call the current vice president and some angry comments about a woman the Internal Revenue Service had sent to investigate his group.

The words certainly sounded like warrior words, fighting words. They sounded full of hate and pride and aggression. It made me think about one of those red sentences, something about the peacemakers being blessed. It made me feel spooky all over again. I wanted to tell Mr. Robertson about it. I wanted to say, "Mr. Robertson, be careful with using those words for war of any kind. Those are fiery, hot words. When you take them into your mouth, they just might burn you."

The Dangers of Hyphenation

It winked from the key pad. It beckoned. It was just waiting to have words wrapped around it.

Let me explain. I was filling out a form for a grant from the North Carolina Arts Council. I was after a wad of folding money from the state with which I intended to free up some time to write poetry. I know that sounds far-fetched, but it's not as bad as taking tax dollars NOT to raise wheat. Like all government forms, the application asked for information that had nothing to do with the subject at hand. It wanted to know what color my skin is, what my ethnic origins are. This apparently bears heavily on the writing of poetry, or fiction, or plays, because the form asked for the information repeatedly.

I got worried about that. Why did it keep asking me? Wasn't I giving the right answers? "Caucasian, just Caucasian," I said. Does the project emphasize the traditions of a particular culture, the form wanted to know. I must not be giving the right answers. It's giving me another chance. I looked over my choices. Since, "the stars, the angels in heaven, the whole enchilada" were not among the choices, I had to rethink my answers.

That's when it happened. I erased my first answer and checked "Other." Then I wrote in Appalachian-American. After all, I'd grown up in the shadows of the Blue Ridge Mountains. At that very moment, I had in my pantry Ball jars full of green beans, squash and deer meat. So I thought I'd just give myself a hyphen.

The form seemed happy. It had more of its blanks filled. Oh, by the way, the form added, I was to send along samples of my work. I would be judged solely on the basis of my work. Solely. My name was not to appear on the poems.

How would the judges know I was Appalachian-American, I fretted? I'm multicultural. They need to know that. Better put in the poem about the mule, and the one about hog killing. Oh yeah, and definitely the one about 'shine making. There, they wouldn't be able to miss it. The packet landed with a solid thud in the mail bin. I grinned. Pretty soon my wallet would be so fat I wouldn't be able to sit straight in a chair.

That's a powerful little piece of punctuation, I said to myself. Powerful. Then I thought about old Tinker Powell, his cheek bulging with a baseball-size chew of Red Man. Powerful was his word. I had on many occasions heard him put it in front of adjectives. But suddenly I was remembering a particular time.

My father and I were standing with Tinker on a rickety wooden bridge over Runnet Bag Creek. The creek bank was crowded with anglers fidgeting with poles and stringers, waiting for noon and the start of trout season. The creek had been stocked with trout from the state hatchery the week before.

The fishermen jockeyed for position near a pool

with an overhanging tree. They were sure that was where all the fish were.

"Damn fools," Tinker said as he studied the fishermen. "Them's government fish that ain't been fed in a week. They're powerful hungry. They'll bite anything."

As if to prove his point, Tinker spat a stream of amber juice and a small chuck of tobacco into the creek. The little wad was struck from underneath as soon as it hit the water.

"That's real fishing," Tinker chuckled. "What fish ain't caught today will die by the end of next week. They don't know how to live in a real creek."

"Noon," someone shouted and all the lines hit the water. Immediately, they started hauling them in. No matter where the lure landed, deep pool or not, it was soon covered by a hungry mouth. I saw one kid stick a pink piece of bubblegum on his hook and reel in a big one. Tinker kept chuckling.

That chuckle is beginning to haunt me. I'm worried. Powerful worried. Must I always be hyphenated? Is there any powder that can rid me of this spot, this flea of a punctuation mark that has designs on my blood? This is what happens when we start pleasing government forms.

Look what a hyphen does to perfectly nice words. Player-coach. Writer-director. Student-athlete. It's the verbal equivalent of Sydney Poitier and Tony Curtis in *The Defiant Ones*, handcuffed together, despising each other. A hyphen makes a phrase look as if it has a weak spot. Pull on both sides and the thing will pop apart.

That's what I had done—introduced a weak spot. And, the worse part was the kin I was trying to claim with that shotgun wedding would have hooted at the idea. The people I know in the mountains need only the two good handles of their given and surname. They wouldn't tolerate a hyphen and neither should a real writer.

A few weeks after that bloated application smacked the bottom of a mail box, I was reading an interview with the Pultizer Prize-winning Poet Laureate of the United States, Rita Dove. She was talking along happily about the things she was writing and then she got to reminiscing about being the only black person in the Iowa Workshop. She said "...[W]hen someone regards you as a hyphenated poet--as an African-American-woman-poet, or a Latin-American-gay-poet, or whatever--then for some reason your peers and the critics start making allowances, the rigor drops; it's this condescension which is so insulting...."

Damn. There was that hyphen again. It was plaguing me. I met a new person at work. He introduced himself as Kevin Walker-Franks. I heard Tinker chuckling.

I promise, Tinker, I promise. I won't rise to that sorry bait again.

The Voices of the People

"I said I was sorry."

"You always say you're sorry. You always say that."

"I am. I am sorry."

One voice was timid, quieted with guilt. The other was tough, fed up.

"I've had it with you."

"I know. Sorry."

This conversation was taking place on one of the gravel paths that skirts the White House grounds. Two men shared the path, myself and a man bundled in what looked like two or three coats. The truly frightening part of this scene is that I wasn't saying a word.

Both voices, terrifying in their different tones and inflections, came from the big man pulling a luggage cart piled with bags, boxes and plastic sheeting. It was quarter to seven in the morning and the trails around the White House were empty except for a few joggers working their way up to the Washington Monument. In the capitol on business, I'd gotten up early to get in a walk before the day's work began. This man, it was obvious, was there because he had nowhere else to be.

I eavesdropped on that conversation almost two years ago, but , as a new election was approaching, I thought often of the man. Not only is he a terribly real example of one of this country's greatest challenges—the caring for, or neglect, of the poor and ill—but he seems to me to embody the split personality that has so characterized our recent elections and maybe, therefore, our nation.

On the one hand there are the angry, venom-spitting attacks of the outraged. On the other are the sympathizing and worrying of the thoughtfully concerned. One side said vote for me because I hate who and what you hate. The other side said vote for me because I care for what you care for. The scary part is that both voices are coming from one entity—the union we call our nation.

Now that we know which representatives and senators, vice-president and president we are sending back to the federal paths around the White House, do we know what we are sending them to do? Are we sending them to hate or to care? Do you think they know?

The man trudged away from me that morning, raging against himself, consumed by his anger and shame. I hoped he wasn't beyond help. I hope we all aren't.

A Poem for the Nation

If your only brush with contemporary American poetry was President Bill Clinton's inauguration in 1993, you might not have been exactly looking forward to the ceremony in 1997.

I had been jubilant when I heard that Clinton was re-instituting the practice of commissioning a poem for his first inauguration. This would be a boon for poetry, giving it a national audience and recognizing its rightful place in public life. I knew there were dozens of poets Clinton could pick who could rise to the occasion and present the nation with a poem that would be both accessible and profound, musical and meaningful. And, indeed, because American poetry is vital—even if it isn't overly visible to mass audiences—there were dozens of poets who would have been up to the task. Unfortunately, Bill Clinton didn't pick one of them.

What we got for an inaugural poem was a nonsensical mishmash of language that made itself ridiculous by trying to be all things to all people. The poem dissolved into a vaporous cloud of good, but ultimately disastrous, equal opportunity intentions.

Michael Chitwood

While Maya Angelou is admired by many readers, her effort to give the tree its due without shorting the rock and the river made images that pulsed to the weave forged in the deep-freezes of hopelessly mixed metaphors.

So to future presidents, I offer this unasked for prescription for the poem to be read before the nation. Make it particular. What we so admire about our Harriet Tubmans, Meriwether Lewises, Martin Luther Kings and even Ted Turners is their cussed individuality. It's their particularities, and peculiarities, that reveal them to be human, and, therefore, like all of us.

Here for example is the unique voice of C.D. Wright, an Arkansas poet who would have made a fine inaugural reader for Clinton's second inauguration but wasn't asked. The words are from her poem, "Our Dust," and sound to me like the whole country singing:

You didn't know my weariness, error, incapacity.
I was the poet
of shadow work and towns with quarter-inch
phone books, of failed
roadside zoos. The poet of yard eggs and
sharpening shops,
jobs at the weapons plant and the Maybelline
factory on the penitentiary road.
....
I never raised your rent. Or anyone else's by God.
Never said I loved you. The future gave me chills.
I used the medium to say: Arise arise and
come together.
Free your children. Come on everybody. Let's start
with Baltimore.

The Unspoiled Past

"Don't spoil it for them. Remember they're kids," my wife admonished as I left the house with my son and his friend. We were on our way to see *Pocahontas,* and I had been grousing from what I had read about the movie. The historical inaccuracies. The wasp-waisted, doe-eyed heroine.

If you grow up in Virginia, you get a big dose of the commonwealth's history, and I've been a nut about Jamestown and Williamsburg ever since elementary school. We even made bus trips to the Tidewater in both fourth and seventh grades.

So imagine my surprise when I saw on the big screen the cartoon representation of that area. Lush, hardwood forests. Crystal streams. A waterfall. I stuffed my mouth with popcorn to keep from ranting to the rapt children sitting beside me.

The actual land of the Jamestwon settlement is just barely above the brackish water of the swampy area around the mouth of the James River. I'd bet there's not a waterfall within a hundred miles. And during the whole movie I didn't see Indian or Englishman slap a mosquito. Yeah, right.

Michael Chitwood

But Disney, as it has proven repeatedly, knows what we want. The Mouse knows Americans aren't interested in history. Some other folks know that too.

In the boil of political rhetoric the coming election is generating, an idea keeps resurfacing. It's on the lips of every wannabe. It goes something like this: "It's time this country (here the PA system reverbs a bit,— country, country, country) got back to its bed rock values (more reverb, —values, values, values.)" Back there, in the past, there was a small town where neighbor helped neighbor, where kids had straight teeth, where everybody had values, family values.

Remember the lunch counters in that town, where *everybody* could go in and enjoy a cherry coke? Remember the schools in that town, where everybody had a chance to learn and on Friday nights at the big game the boys learned sportsmanship and the girls cheered. If the girls were lucky, real lucky, they'd marry Mr. Football. And remember the churches—Baptist, Methodist, Presbyterian, it didn't matter—they all supported each other's *pork* barbeques. Remember those sweet, uncomplicated days? Remember those values?

It's all back there. And, all we've got to do is return. All we've got to do is pack our bags and head to that wonderful place where the water was crystal clear, and it fell in musical tones down to deep pools. And here's the best part, ladies and gentleman, in that whole town, in that entire sleepy little town, there's not a single mosquito.

Bread and Circuses

I suddenly had a queasy feeling, a kind of vertigo. The floor was strewn with ripped Christmas paper, presents were stacked beside their recipients, and the adults were watching the children give half-hearted hugs to the grandparents.

But there was a catch. Now the adults *and* children were watching the adults watch the children give the hugs. My brother-in-law's new camcorder had captured the holiday festivities, and here we were watching, less than a quarter hour after the events. I felt trapped in a Norman Rockwell *Saturday Evening Post* cover. You know the one—where the artist is painting a picture of the artist painting a picture of the artist. It repeats itself in ever decreasing miniatures until it vanishes.

"We just did this," I said. "Why are we watching it?"

"Don't be a grump," my sister said. "Look at the kids."

Sure enough the kids were fascinated with their images. They called out their own names each time they appeared on the screen. Here was the ultimate

Michael Chitwood

self-portrait, I thought. One in which each life event has an almost immediate visual echo.

The queasy feeling came back the other night as I watched a basketball game. It was one of those huge, domed arenas, the latest thing, the kind of place the Romans would have been proud of. There were four giant screens above the court to show the folks at the game what the folks at home were seeing. (Is there something wrong with this picture?)

There was a break in the action, and the courtside cameraman panned the crowd. That's camera talk. Pan. It used to mean to "criticize severely." Anyway, the camera zooms in on this guy who thrusts his index finger in the air and leers at the camera. Then he does a strange thing. He forgets the camera and checks himself out on the big screen. It was as if he had to make sure he was there. "ALLLLL-RIIIIIIGHT," he mouths.

He was anonymously famous—his face above the crowd big as a risen moon. And now he was staring at himself, a moon mooning over itself. I can just hear him the next day.

"Did'ja see me, man? Huge. I must've been on a hundred thousand, no, three hundred thousand TVs."

"Hey who won the game?" his friend asks.

"Game? Game? Didn't you see me? Big. Big as life."

Bread and circuses? If the Romans had developed video technology, we'd all be saying, "Hail, Caesar."

Whispers

It was unusual, but we didn't pay too much attention. Paul's dad showed up at our campsite on Saturday afternoon and huddled for a while with the two scout leaders. The assistant scoutmaster stayed on the creek bank with us, in case any of our fledging trout fishermen fell in.

The rest of the day was routine, which meant that four of us eventually did fall in and the rest of us thrashed so in the water of the shallow creek that nobody caught many fish.

We checked the duty roster and complained about who would be cooking. The idea was that we would learn independence and responsibility, which meant that our meals were heavily seasoned with ashes. We weren't the most meticulous cooks, and a campfire isn't the most precise cooking instrument, so things occasionally got pretty rough. The assistant scoutmaster, however, would stir up a stew or some mashed potatoes and make sure that everybody got at least one dish that wasn't charred beyond recognition.

The four boys who were scheduled to wash

dishes protested bitterly, as the boys scheduled to wash dishes always did. But the assistant scoutmaster helped them out and got the job taken care of quickly.

Then we chose sides for a game of capture the flag. While we rampaged through the pasture and along the creek, the leaders sipped coffee by the campfire. Two more boys went in the creek. A tent collapsed when someone tripped on the support ropes.

Around ten, the scoutmasters announced that it was time for us to hit the hay. Now this was odd. They usually didn't call taps on us until midnight or after. "Everybody into their tents," they announced. "Has everybody got a partner? Everybody needs a partner."

Again, this was unusual. They had never been concerned in the past about who was sleeping where, or if *any* sleeping was going on. But we obeyed, we *were* boy scouts after all, and turned in two by two to our pup tents.

The assistant tidied up the cooking gear and went to his tent. The two leaders then came to every tent and in whispers said, "If you hear any rustling around your tent tonight, yell for us, okay?" Rustling? What did they mean? Was something dangerous going on?

My tent mate and I discussed what the threat could be. Had Paul's dad brought news of a bear sighting or an escaped convict?

The news that Paul's dad had brought, I found out much later, was that some rumors were circulating that the assistant scoutmaster was gay. The man that had for three years been a trusted influence suddenly became something to whisper about, something to fear.

The long dark hours crawled by. But there was no rustling. Everyone woke unharmed, including the three boys who were so frightened by the unnamed fear that they sought out the assistant scoutmaster's tent, where they passed the night protected from the unspeakable.

Y

I've got this Y chromosome. It's now cost me two jobs, and danged if I don't think it's starting to be a liability.

The chromosome is what, at the instant of conception, turned me into a male. Little did I suspect as an embryo, that this pesky chromosome would someday be a vital part of my resume.

Here's what has happened so far. Last year, a friend of mine decided she was leaving her teaching position at a state university. They would need someone to start in the middle of the year. She thought I'd be perfect for the job. She recommended me. When the news got out, her friend who chairs the Women's Studies Department called her and said, "This is terrible. You know what they'll do, don't you? They'll hire a man."

But it turns out that the Women's Studies Department had someone coming in who had a little experience teaching writing, much less experience and fewer publications than I had, according to my open-minded female friend. One week and some serious lobbying later, my Y chromosome struck.

Then this spring, I was all lined up for a job next fall at another North Carolina university. It looked like a shoe-in. Then suddenly another candidate appeared. Our qualifications were similar, so a departmental vote was taken. The vote was a dead tie, according to the gentleman who called me late one night to bring me the bad news. "Other considerations" came into play, he said. It turns out that the winning candidate is the fiancée of someone on the university faculty. The department is heavily male, and she's a loved one. Good-bye job number two.

Well, white boy, it's time, I hear a chorus saying. And, I have to admit that's probably true. For years, that Y chromosome landed people a lot of jobs, and being someone's cousin or nephew didn't hurt either.

But I never realized justice would feel like this. Like a ten-penny nail being driven into your gut. What we don't understand when we talk about the idea of justice is that ultimately, it's personal on both sides of the scales.

The trick, for me now, is not to get bitter. My head says this is fair, but you know how your head can tell you one thing and the rest of you has to go out and run two miles. I know bitterness eats you like a cancer. I know that, so I won't think about this again. Yeah, right.

I have one help in this: I love women. I married one. My mother's one. Several of my best friends are women. So, I'll just get my running shoes on for now and say to the winning candidates: congratulations, work hard and be cheerful about it.

Questions

"Dad?"

I heard the question mark at the end of the simple syllable. Only your own child can pack a single word with so much ominous cargo. The four-year-old voice was sweet, but I heard it coming. This was going to be one of those questions that roll from an innocent mouth and pin a parent to the wall.

"Dad, are we Jewish or Curstin?" It was early December and obviously the talk in my son's day care was of the different religious traditions that would be celebrated in the coming season. Well, at least I *know* the answer to this one, I thought. But I stumbled as I tried to reply.

"Curstin," I finally said, using the humor of my boy's mispronunciation to lighten the situation for me.

Mercifully, he seemed satisfied, but I spent the rest of that evening, and many evenings since, wrestling with the answer. I think it's going to be a life-long, no-holds-barred, Texas grudge match.

I grew up in a rural Methodist church, literally grew up. I mean from the time I could walk until I could walk away from it, at about the age of sixteen, that church was a big part of my family's life. I was "saved" at age twelve by a Muslim-turned-Christian evangelist who wept before the congregation, because he would never see his parents again. They had died Muslim, you see, and he now knew he would not find them on the shores of Glory. At the beginning of the second drag through "Just As I Am," I went down the aisle.

It only took about a week for the theatrics of the revival to wear off and leave me feeling downright foolish. The wars of my adolescence were largely Crusades—Mom and Dad bearing the standard of the cross and me waving Kurt Vonnegut and Albert Camus novels.

But now I have to admit that I can't leave this Christian business alone. Call it a childhood infection. Yeah, Falwell, Swaggert, Baker and company have made a mockery of it. With their tearful confessions and crude television dunning, they've taken away much of its sacred language. And yet...

And yet, I keep seeing my grandmother making her way to the humming Frigidaire. One of the two fat men in dark suits who made regular visits was taking up her love seat all by himself. He held a large leather book. He was either the insurance man or the Baptist preacher; I got them confused. They looked alike. Grandma dug the bills out of the vegetable bin, her version of the safe deposit box, and handed them over. The man wrote her name in the book and then stamped "Paid" beside it.

But which man was it? Why did she seem so comforted? It's something a little boy wants to know.

Old Virginny

No more "Carry Me Back to Old Virginny." The Senate of my native state recently voted to retire "Old Virginny," the official state song, because some of the song's verses contain language that people find to be racially offensive. The old song, it seems, is the musical equivalent of the stars and bars flying over the South Carolina capitol building.

Now, I have to admit that it's hard not to hear the racial insult in lines like, "There's where the old darkey's heart am longed to go. That's where I laboured so hard for old massa." It doesn't matter that the writer is saying *despite* the hardships and injustice suffered there, he still longs for Old Virginny. And it doesn't really matter that the song was written by a black minstrel. Not many people know that, and even if you did you could argue that the man had just bought into the racism of his era.

But here's my question. Did they have to junk the whole song? Okay, they didn't actually junk it; they declared it "official state song emeritus." It's hard not to laugh just saying that phrase. What does that mean, that the song gets retirement benefits or something?

But why do away with the whole song in the first place? I mean, it's got what you want a state song to have—nostalgia, sloppy sentimentality, mentions of the state's agricultural products. If it could have just worked in a list of all the presidents that were Virginia natives, it would be the perfect state song.

So here's my modest proposal to the Virginia legislature. Don't scrap the whole song. Just change the offending lines. That's become accepted practice with the old blood-drenched church hymns that incorrectly refer to the masculinity of God. If we can whip our hymns into shape, why not just tinker with a state song a bit?

You could even kill two birds with one stone by replacing the insensitive lines with Ebonics, thus eliminating the problem while celebrating cultural diversity. How about "That's where the homies am hanging, watching out for The Man"? Or something like that. It's much better, don't you think?

You know, now that I think about it, the dogwood really isn't much of a state tree. I mean, it doesn't say twenty-first century. How about the satellite dish. That would be so much more modern....

Life Lessons

Biology Lab • The Pretender • Away from the Crowd • The Life of the Mind • A Certain Slant of Light (November) • Outdoor Wedding • Magic Kingdom • How a Kid Gets in a Car • Teachers • The Three A.M. Stare • The Names • That Time of Day

Biology Lab

The class was Advanced Biology, which was very appropriate given what we high school juniors and seniors were feeling. Most of our waking thoughts, at least the boys' anyway, were focused on advancing biology as far as our dates and fears would allow.

Because this college-bound group had worked hard and taken our assignments seriously, we had earned a treat, the teacher announced. We were going on a field trip—to the state college with its collection of human cadavers.

On the bus trip over, our teacher explained that a graduate student would conduct our tour and that one of the cadavers had been readied for us to inspect. We were to remember that we were representatives of our school and, for the sake of future students who would want to make this trip, we were to conduct ourselves maturely and pay close attention to the graduate student.

Paying close attention was going to be no trouble, I knew, as soon as we were introduced to our graduate student. She was twenty-two or -three, funny, shapely, smart. In other words, the stuff of dreams. She spoke to us as equals. I was in heaven.

She briefly discussed where the cadavers had come from and then lead us over to "our" body. It looked more like an ancient leather box than a human. It took close inspection to discern whether it was male or female. It reeked of formaldehyde.

Our guide introduced us to "Henry." She said the students gave each body a name, and she chatted a little about Henry's life as she pulled on surgical gloves. Then she blithely spread Henry's ribcage and invited us to examine the chest cavity.

My eyes watered from the pungent cloud wafting off Henry. Through the blur, I studied a body that still breathed. She discussed Henry's probable cause of death, noted anomalies of his organs, pointed out interesting features.

As she became more engrossed in what she was saying, she leaned closer to Henry. I don't recall what she was saying, because as I watched, the tiny chain around her neck swung free. Its small gold figurine gently brushed Henry's lips. In the instant that the long-dead man kissed her charm, I caught a staggering blend of his and her perfumes.

The Pretender

College boy on a summer job, I spent three months looking down on the workers of the Angle Plant of J.P. Stevens, Inc. My job, for most of June, July and August, was to change the long fluorescent tubes that threw light on the Draper looms roaring out yard after yard of white cloth. I rode a wobbly scaffolding over the looms and the heads of the weavers, cloth doffers and fixers. *Dim bulbs*, I thought. *I'm spending my break with dim bulbs.*

At school that year I had been introduced to a singer named Jackson Browne. Young, mournful and full of longing, I played him in my head as I popped out the dying tubes. The looms at full throttle filled the room with a gigantic static; it was like a constant tidal wave. The earplugs protected our hearing and made any kind of conversation impossible. From my perch, as I swiped Fantastic on the tin light shades, I pitied those country folk, voluntarily deaf, grubbing from payday to payday, all of them with the "heart and soul of the spender" that Jackson Browne kept singing about in my head.

At the end of the day, they would flood out through

the narrow door in the brick wall, blinking in the glare of the four o'clock summer sun they hadn't seen all day. Many were headed for another four or five hours of work, planting tobacco, cutting hay, getting water to the beef cattle. After work, Colin, the man I rode with, would sit on a low wooden bench, patting his face and neck with a damp paper towel, talking with a few others about fishing, softball or how many times the yard had needed mowing that summer. I shifted from one foot to the other. I never sat down. I didn't want him to think I wanted to while away the rest of my day.

As the workers walked the aisles between the looms, filaments of yarn drifted in their wake. They looked like tiny, nearly invisible tentacles, catching on their pants and skirts, binding them to this roaring room, to the silence of their working lives.

"You got a minute," Colin said as we drove home. *Probably wants to show me his yard*, I thought. "Sure," I said.

We drove down to an old barn near his house. He motioned for me to climb the ladder up to the loft. I gingerly tested each rung and poked my head through the hole in the floor of the loft. Surprised, a buzzard spread her black wings and hissed at me. She stood her ground over the nest, which erupted with bald, pink heads. I ducked back through the floor pumped on the adrenaline the big wings and snake-like hiss had given me.

"How'd you find them," I asked. I couldn't imagine someone climbing that ladder just to be poking around.

"I heard them rustling," he said picking strands of yarn from his pants. He rolled them into a ball and flipped them into the dark of the barn. "I was just down here listening," he said.

I pushed my rickety scaffolding toward September, ready to get on with my life. Ready to be away from those dim bulbs. I had grown used to the earplugs, Jackson Browne and my political science and sociology class thoughts playing over and over in my head.

You can wait years for life to begin, or you can listen for the rustling.

Away from the Crowd

After we canoed the first lake and portaged to the next, we might go the rest of the trip without seeing any other people, we told each other as we got the boats off the car and paid the man we'd hired to transport us to our remote launching point. We'd come a long way, from North Carolina and Virginia, to Algonquin Park, Canada. We wanted the wilderness experience.

Everything we would use for the next five days, we carried in four packs. "Self-reliant, Emerson's envy," I quipped to my three companions as we paddled onto Magnetawan Lake, heading for the carry to the Petawawa River. The exotic names were a wild elixir in our mouths.

Dan pointed to a red-tailed hawk. "It'll take us two days to get to Burntroot, but he'll be there in...." The hawk drifted out of sight on cue. "Hell, he's there now," Dan finished the modified quote from *Jeremiah Johnson,* one of our favorite movies, which we had been quoting liberally on the trip up.

We pulled the named creeks, rivers and lakes under our canoes, checking the provincial park map for the next portages, which were conveniently marked with bright yellow signs.

Around our first campfire, as I was about to recite a line of Thoreau's, I suddenly felt surrounded. I realized that the dark of the Canadian forest, at least our part of it, was crowded. All day we had filtered the sky's blue, the swish of the paddles' little whirlpools, the alarm of the jay, through other people's eyes and ears. From Hollywood to Hemingway, we were quoting our way through the woods. After traveling more than seven hundred miles, we were getting our wilderness second-hand.

All the next day I worried that thought like a loose button. How was I to get away from this crowd in my head? Could I? I tried not to make any literary references.

The packs seemed heavier and the lakes longer on the second day, but the evening sky was so clear we decided, tired as we were, to drift out and watch the stars come out. The sun did a slow fade and the stars were pale at first, shy, it seemed, to enter our gossipy zodiac. We called out constellations we recognized, but then as all surrounding light disappeared and the lake vanished and the trees and shoreline, we floated silently with those bone-white sparks. The Milky Way was a bright smear, but our astronomy had stopped. The stars formed new clusters. Occasionally, one seared across the darkness. My shoulders burned with the knowledge of where I was. Overhead, nameless by the thousands, the stars were the stars.

The Life of the Mind

I don't know why we'd gone to the pool. It was one of those unnecessary swimming pools, like the ones you see at beach-front hotels. I mean, there's the whole mysterious, throbbing ocean, and some people want to splash in chlorinated toddler pee.

Anyway, this pool was beside a large lake where the water was brown, changing to deep green in the depths. Ski boats whizzed by. There was the possibility of seeing a snapping turtle or snake. There was the possibility of seeing two drunk boat drivers slam their boats together. Anything could happen.

So, why we had chosen, on this particular July afternoon, to sizzle beside a campground swimming pool the size of a small living room, I can not say. Of course, my date and I were teenagers, which could explain anything. I recall that we had some vague notion that the pool was more cosmopolitan, more *with it*. The pool would be quiet. We could read our books and think. We were thinking a lot. We were asking serious questions.

When I first glanced up from my book, the little girl seemed to be playing some kind of solitary game.

She was eleven, maybe twelve, stick thin. She would sink to the bottom of the pool, bounce and then surface. When she came to the top of the water, she stretched out both arms in a languid motion. Her face was blank. I think it was the fact that she was so lost in her thoughts, in her imagined ballet, that kept me watching her. I was attracted to the life of the mind that was going on in the deep end of this tiny pool. With each surfacing, her left hand missed the side of the pool only by inches.

As I watched, I noticed that her bounces were beginning to be less forceful. Her head was not clearing the water, but her expression remained placid. I think she could not believe what was happening to her.

A middle-aged man in a white shirt, dress slacks, white socks and black wingtip shoes realized that the girl was actually in trouble at the same moment I did. I entered the pool from the right side and caught the girl around the waist. He had committed himself from the left and couldn't stop when he saw that I already had her. He flew over our heads, landing halfway across the small pool.

I sat the girl on the side of the pool and only then did her expression change. She began to cry, and relatives appeared from every direction. The well-dressed rescuer climbed the ladder and looked at me.

"She was drowning," he said.

"At first, I thought she was playing," I said.

What we had said didn't seem to satisfy either of us, but neither of us could think of anything else. I returned to my towel, but I left the book splayed where it had fallen.

I started to shake. The water in the pool seemed

Michael Chitwood

to jump. The glare was intense. I had to squint. Water squirted from the man's wingtips as he walked away. I started to laugh. I laughed so hard I could hardly catch my breath.

A Certain Slant of Light (November)

You don't generally hear it discussed around the office coffee pot. You don't get updates on it from the TV news. Newspapers don't print maps showing its direction and strength. In fact, it's usually confined to the conversations of painters, poets and religious mystics, but this time of year it flexes its muscle. This time of year it gets serious.

I'm talking about that "certain slant of light/ winter afternoons," as Emily Dickinson put it. She captured in words, as Edward Hopper and others have captured in paint, the way light, even though it has no weight or smell or sound, can become a physical presence in our lives.

I first learned the lesson as a kid playing night games of hide and seek. Base was in the front yard, a tree washed by the white glare of a powerful floodlight. The light was angled down the side of the house and created a wall of darkness at the back corner. It was as though a huge black panel had been erected there, and it seemed as solid as the side of the brick house. As whoever was "it" began to count, I would run full-tilt toward that darkness. The thrill of plung-

Michael Chitwood

ing from the light into its absence, completely unable to see what waited beyond, always went through me like a whiff of ammonia.

It's a spiritual lesson. That something without form or heft can stop traffic, cause accidents, maim. That this light is both dramatically beautiful and actually dangerous makes it even more appealing, I think. It shows what painters, poets and mystics have always known—that the light is not metaphorical, and our journey in it is not allegorical. It's real and dangerous, and we must pay careful attention, and sometimes even that won't be enough.

This is the only time of year when we all are privileged to see like the great painters, to observe almost against our will the way the common world is illuminated.

It's "an imperial affliction/ Sent us of the Air," Ms. Dickinson says. "When it comes, the Landscape listens—."

Outdoor Wedding

"Isn't this perfect?" one of the guests was saying. "I mean, it's just the right reflection of the meaning of a marriage. This calm, beautiful spot where two people come together and are comforted."

Okay, I'll admit the little grove of oak trees on the grassy knoll was pleasant and you could barely hear the traffic sluicing by outside the park's borders. But this woman was laying it on a bit thick, I thought. "Relationship book overload," I whispered to my wife who shot me one of her don't-be-a-jerk looks.

But the ceremony was about to begin so I was denied the opportunity to hear any more observation on the metaphorical significance of the landscape as it relates to the nature of marriage. I hated that because I always think it's so nice when nature obliges us by being metaphorical.

Anyway the bride made it over the somewhat rough path to where the preacher and groom stood without incident, and the standing group of onlookers tightened around the happy couple now facing a makeshift altar.

The minister began his duties, and, at the same

Michael Chitwood

time, a group of eight to ten squirrels decided to visit the canopy of new leaves over our heads. At first, it was just a bough shaking here and there and an occasional scrap of bark fluttering down. But as the ceremony wore on, the squirrels began a game of rodent tag that soon had twigs and bark showering the crowd. In a train that looked like tiny, furry roller coaster cars, they were tearing through the tree tops, up trunks, out along limbs and, when they reached the flimsy tips of branches, they'd make wild leaps to the next tree.

Now you can never be sure how people in a wedding party are going to react when unexpected events intrude on their special hour. I've seen brides crumble into tears because a baby was crying during the exchanging of the vows. I've seen grooms cut hot looks at mothers weeping in the front pew.

In this case, the bride was beginning to giggle. A good sign. We'll be okay, I thought, if the minister steps on it. But then, one of the daredevil squirrels misjudged a leap. He clutched at a twig, curled and plunged into the on-lookers, striking a distinguished looking gentlemen in a nice blue suit squarely in the chest. I'm not sure who was more surprised, the man or the squirrel now swinging on his coat front. The man began a kind of slow rumba, backing out of the crowd with his eyes locked on the squirrel. The squirrel seemed to shake himself, regained his composure and then leapt to the ground and scampered off.

The bride and groom were laughing hysterically. Well, I thought, they'll be all right. When real life comes crashing in on their metaphors, they'll know how to handle it.

Magic Kingdom

Through the entrance arches we could see shrubs that had been meticulously clipped to resemble dancing hippos in tutus. The diesel-powered tram chugged to a stop with its capacity load of camera-laden tourists, and the PA crackled with the announcement: "This is the Magic Kingdom."

My wife and I had decided that it was time for our seven-year-old to have the All-American experience—the spring break trip to Disney World. It seemed like such a good idea back in January when we started cooking it up. Unfortunately, it had also seemed like a good idea to about forty million other people back in January, and now they were all here, on this one tram from the parking lot named Goofy, which I was beginning to understand as an extremely appropriate beginning for the experience.

But I resolved to be cheerful and patient for our son's sake. I resolved this after my wife threatened to remove one of my ears with her fingernail file if I made any more cracks about knowing how cattle feel on the way to the slaughterhouse.

So suddenly tolerant and good-humored, I

Michael Chitwood

planned for adventures that would fire a seven-year-old's imagination. Over the next five days, we did find a few. The Haunted Mansion stills lives in family conversations, and the Star Tours ride, a real corker that uses pilot flight training technology, gets revisited quite a bit.

But there's one attraction at the Disney/MGM park that is plaguing my thoughts. It could be that our visit to this show came on the last day of the trip, and even my determined *esprit de corps* (I still have both ears) was wearing thin. For whatever reason, as the *Indiana Jones* and the *Raiders of the Lost Ark* show began, I found myself feeling a little nauseous. A perky young woman in khaki safari shorts came out and introduced herself as the production manager for this "shoot." We were about to be shown how some of the fabulous stunts of the *Indiana Jones* movie were done. Cameramen lugged in their bazooka-sized equipment and set up for the various angles. We were introduced to the technical crew, stunt trainers and demolition experts. And, for the next ten minutes, they tried very hard to convince us that they were the stunt doubles and acrobats and that this was how the movie was done.

What was so bothersome to me was the feeling that this was the next evolutionary step for our fantasy lives. The screens of our lives—the big one in the darkened theater, the medium-sized one of the TV, and the small one of the computer—have become our reality. And so, we're willing to entertain a fantasy about them. We don't imagine what it would be like to be the Swiss Family Robinson; we imagine what it would be like to be the people who play the people that are playing the parts of made-up characters in a story. Is this disdain for fantasy or acknowledgment of a complete immersion in virtual reality?

I don't know, but I was glad to get back to a real parking lot and drive a real car away into a mundane, but thoroughly real afternoon.

How a Kid Gets in a Car

The meeting has been scheduled for three weeks. People have rearranged their plans to be there. It's the only time this group of people can get together and nothing can move forward until people hash things out at this meeting.

Now, all you have to do is get your child out of the house and into the car. Children have a sense about things like this. When you absolutely *have* to be somewhere, children will become interested in how their shoe strings work. They will unlace, completely, both shoes in order to conduct further studies of this important phenomenon.

"Dad, look at this. You have to skip a hole when you cross over."

It's really inspiring, isn't it, how kids are just fascinated by the world? Okay, you've got the shoes on; the lunch bag is packed, and you're all the way to the car door. If there's not too much traffic at school, you'll make it.

Your child opens the door and starts to examine the place where the seat and the seat back meet. "Oh gross, a French fry," your child cries and immediately picks up the fry. "How old is this?"

The half-life of a fast food French fry is about three years, so this one could be from the Bush administration.

"Can I eat it?"

"No, get in."

"What should I do with it?" the inquiring little mind wants to know. "I know, I'll see if the cat will eat it."

Before you can react, the miniature scientist is off, fry pinched between index finger and thumb, to find kitty.

"Wait, just get in," you bawl.

But Chucky Darwin is gone. At this point, you should reflect on the hectic nature of our lives. You should long for a simpler time, a time when parents took a few extra minutes to allow youngsters to explore their world. It was a time when children learned from the slow rhythm of the seasons, when whole days could be spent observing the subtle changes each day brings.

Wait a minute. This kid is wearing a VR Ranger t-shirt. His cruising will be done on the Internet. He's clutching a fossil French fry.

"Get...in....the...car."

"How are French fries harvested?"

Isn't that exciting, the vivid imagination, the ranging intellect, the probing mind? Couldn't you just strangle them?

Teachers

When someone does her a kindness, a special favor that can't really be repaid in earthly currency, my grandmother will say, "I thank you 'til you're better paid." It comes, I guess, from a time when neighbors helped each other with work and no money ever changed hands, just appreciation and an obligation to pass it on.

That phrase came to mind after my son went to his pre-kindergarten doctor's visit. The doctor was kindly and made Jacob laugh while doing his physical exam. He looked in Jacob's ears and eyes, thumped his back, tapped on his knees and ankles with the little rubber hammer, efficiently went through the exam and jotted a few notes into the record. The whole process lasted about fifteen minutes.

When we went out to settle up with the young woman who handles the financial end of this rite of passage, I watched her write $54 in the space beside PE 5 to 11, code 308. In modern health care terminology, code 308, Physical Exam, 5 to 11, means that a quarter hour of the doctor's time is worth $54.

Well, that's the way it is, I thought. Then I thought about Ms. Jul. Her name is Julie, and she was Jacob's primary caretaker when he entered day care. He was three months old, and Ms. Julie held him, fed him, changed his diapers, sang to him and rocked him to sleep. When he began to talk, his infant tongue could only handle the first part of her name, and she became Ms. Jul to all of us. Then came Ms. Carolyn, Ms. Sharon, Ms. April, Ms. Paula, Mr. Bryan, Ms. Christi, Ms. Teresa, Mr. David and Ms. Melissa. They rubbed his back to get him to sleep, listened to his endless ramblings about Megazord at Show and Tell, taught him to sing and recorded his descriptions of his paintings: "A bear in his cave and the black is the door and the yellow is his toy donkey." That one's framed and on our wall. Mr. David got him to eat lettuce. Ms Paula taught him to bowl. They spent hours, days, weeks with him.

They did all this for less than $216 an hour, considerably less. When school starts, other teachers will help Jacob learn to write, read, add, subtract, explore history, chemistry, geography, all at considerably less than $216 an hour.

Maybe the people who teach and care for our children need some codes. Code 919, rubbing backs. Code C12, putting bandaid on booboo. 456, getting four-year-olds to share.

What should kindness, patience, generosity of spirit be worth per hour? I don't know, but it's more than what it's going for these days.

It's not as good as a code 308, and I know it buys damn few groceries, but to Jacob's teachers, past and future, I say I thank you 'til you're better paid.

The Three A.M. Stare

Has it all come back to you? That's been the re-current question, always from other parents, since our daughter was born, and there's always a silent acknowledgment behind the question that had your memory been completely intact nine months ago you might not have signed up for this task. It's a wry, good-natured joke between compatriots, like those salty drill sergeants who constantly complain about military life and then re-enlist every time.

So we've re-upped after eight years, and, yeah, it's all come back to me. Not that you have a choice about that. When someone starts screaming in your bedroom at two A.M., it's not like you can say, "Oh, I didn't remember this part so I think I'll just ignore it."

And actually, it's the fact that you can't ignore newborns that makes us give them their proper due. I mean, if you viewed these brand new humans in the sentimental gift card kind of way, you would be tempted to think of them only as "bundles of joy" and "precious angels come to earth." Now don't get me wrong, when they're lying in the crib sleeping, they are everything the cards proclaim them to be—

which is to say, one-dimensional embodiments of the best of being human. They are unspeakably beautiful, fragile and innocent.

But what I think all parents are acknowledging when they ask if it's "*ALL*" come back is what happens when these gorgeous creatures in the crib open their eyes.

Now, I'm not talking about the crying, though that's an undeniable part of the first several months. And I'm not talking about the sleeplessness, which in combination with the crying can turn a reasonable, self-assured, mature adult into a trembling, jumpy, irritable mess. But, because this is our second child, I know you get over this.

No, what's just recently come back to me is the terrifying nature of a calm infant's gaze.

Contrary to what you might think you remember, there's nothing innocent about a newborn's steely stare. Believe me, an eight-year-old can give you looks that break your heart with vulnerability. But a newborn looks at you with the eyes of God. Particularly if it's three A.M.

Here is a blue, searching stare that says, "What are you to me?" "What *will* you be to me?" "Will you be able to love me enough; will I you?"

When those nearly translucent eyelids open, they reveal not just a "bundle of joy" but a complex, demanding, intelligent entity. They unleash a fierce gaze, and it's takes the fiercest kind of love to return that frank look.

The Names

The phrase followed me home. The woman who takes care of our new daughter had spoken it innocently, but as I drove away from her house I couldn't get it out of my mind.

"She's a good girl," our experienced caregiver had said. "The second child is usually more relaxed." The second child. Well, there are two children in our house now, and for that I'm grateful and happy. But this good little girl is not the second child.

There are two distinctly different things I'll always remember about the second child. The first is that moment in the ultrasound room, my wife on the table staring at the ceiling, the technician looking to the screen, prodding my wife's abdomen, once, twice, a third time. I could see the fetus on the gray and black screen. I could make out the eyes, the nose, the mouth, one hand. And I could see, and knew before the technician said coolly, "There's no heartbeat."

The noise—noise is as close as I can come to describing it—that came spontaneously from my wife was unearthly. It was a pure animal noise, a noise beyond reason or consolation. I keep that scene and sound now like a scar in my memory.

The other thing about the second child, though, is the names. When you're expecting a baby you collect names. From business cards, book spines, photograph captions, shouts from the playground, the red script over the mechanic's heart. You gather them and try them out, imagining them said in joy and anger. How would it be to say this one a thousand times, to call it into a darkening neighborhood? To call and then, when the response comes to add, "Suppertime, come on."

What will kindergartners shorten it to? What nicknames might come out of it? Is it a good, strong, confident name?

There were enough names, girls' and boys', released into that ultrasound room to make a whole classroom. Let's say they're second graders, fidgety, giggling, promising. Let's say they're whispering secrets that, some time or other, will be told to us so that we will understand such things. Let's say they know we think of them.

That Time of Day

The caregiver is cheerful. She tells me what a great day my child has had. My daughter has been smiling, cooing and snoozing happily in the swing. "Great," I say, while I pack up her numerous clothes and food items. I say the good-byes, get her loaded into the car seat and then make the tricky merge into the creeping afternoon traffic on Interstate 40.

I turn and say something reassuring to my daughter and she, reassured, begins to cry. First a whimper. Then the tune-up. Then the red-faced, head-back wailing. Traffic crawls. The guy in the car inching along beside me is singing, rocking to the happy beat of a song I can only imagine. The woman I can see in the rearview mirror is talking into her cell phone. She laughs at some joke. My daughter has attained the shrill "uh-wa, uh-wa" scream-chant that she can keep up for the entire commute. I know she can do it. She's done so several times.

This is the beginning of the five-to seven-o'clock gauntlet, as I've come to call it. It's the time of day when I fully understand William Butler Yeats line of poetry about the center not holding. The center has disintegrated absolutely. My daughter's day-long happy face has become the model for Munch's *The Scream* painting. My son, whom we'll pick up from school soon, will sullenly ask what we're having for dinner. It's not pizza. He won't be happy.

"Hey, at least, you're *having* dinner," my internal social worker, shouts to me. "Quit your yuppie whining," the worker continues. "Nobody held a gun to your head and made you have children. You got on this train joyously and you know you're not sorry. Besides, don't you know this is a compliment to you. Your children are polite and happy all day long. In your presence, they feel protected, at ease. They can decompress. They can vent the steam they've stored up all day."

Great, because she knows I love her, my daughter can cry for the next thirty minutes. My son can put his forehead on the passenger side window and observe that, "We never have anything good for dinner." Yeah, I feel the love!

When we pick up my son, he recites his lines perfectly as we drive home. Then I pull into the driveway and there's the bicycle, right where I'd asked him not to leave it. I brake, but before I can say a word or even cut my eyes murderously toward my son, he pipes, "Sorry, I'll get it, Dad." He hops out and moves the bike, then gives me an exaggerated traffic cop wave. He's smiling. My shoulders relax. Without the previous forty minutes, I wouldn't have been ready for this graceful moment. I would have missed it on an easier day.

"Okay," I tell my social worker, "okay, I'll take it from here."

Blood Kin

Naming Names

When she wants to call my name, she backs up about eighty years and gets a running start. Frank, James, Trobie, TW...aw...Michael. Finally, there I am at the end of this invisible line.

It's not that my grandmother's memory is that bad—she recently gave a little talk on her church's first hundred years. It's just that she has a lot of people in her head now, and she has to sort through them to get to me.

It used to bother me. In the small town where I grew up, you were constantly reminded of whose boy you were, as if that explained you.

"You're T.W. and Elaine's oldest, aren't you?"

"Is Flukie Hall your uncle?"

"Aren't you kin to those Chitwoods that live over near Blackwater?"

Yes. Yes. Yes. I'd have to say. In the throes of adolescence, I always wanted to scream, "What of it? What difference does it make? I'm different from all of them."

Of course, *I Am* is the teenage war cry, and that's as it should be.

Michael Chitwood

But when it comes time to paint the inside of a house you've just bought, or take care of a newborn, or get through a serious operation, you find being somebody's boy is a handy thing.

I love to hear her call the roll now. After each name, I can almost hear them answer. "Here." "Present." "Yeah." "I'm listening." She throws in everybody, the long-dead to the newly arrived. The illiterate and the over-educated. The diligent and the deadbeats. The line marches out of the past, troops up to me and then goes on to my younger brother, my son.

Of course, it puzzles my young son. He doesn't understand why his great-grandmother thinks of him as so many people. But sometimes, alone in the car, I do it myself now. Out loud. I call them down out of the air. The whole tribe, good and bad, because I know they're mine and, somehow, they're rooting for me.

Open Letter

She would read it for me, give me it's information. It told her when to plant potatoes, when to can peaches, when it would snow. Whether it was full, quarter or just a silver sliver, the moon spoke to my grandmother and she would translate its ancient language for me.

After mowing her yard, or raking some leaves, she liked to sit out on her porch and enjoy her day's accomplishment. And I couldn't wait for the moon to show itself and reveal whatever portent it had for us. We would watch it brighten as the evening fell and then she'd say, "See that halo around the moon and the three stars inside. That means we'll have rain in three days."

I never remembered to check the accuracy of her predictions. That someone could read the sky seemed a wonder beyond the necessity of proof.

When I went away to college, she would write to me and ask if I'd seen the moon on a particular day. "The full moon, did you see it? It was near about bright as day that night."

And the truth was I would have seen it. She'd

Michael Chitwood

trained me, and suddenly reading the shaky words she'd penned I'd realize that on that night, walking back to my room from the library, I had taken notice, even stopped to watch the fat, gold globe seem to sail through a cloud bank.

These days she calls after a bright full moon. "Did you see that one? I was thinking you did."

Now I know that here at the end of the twentieth century we're done with getting signs and lessons from the moon. This is the information age. We fax. We e-mail. The moon is a cold rock we've explored and are finished with. We've been there, done that. The moon is passé. And it's been used in so many poems and rhymed with June so many times that it can't be pressed into literary service. It's signified all it can. And even the oldest hippies have given up planting potatoes.

It's time to move on. Time to download the calico and get over the old-fashioned, grandmotherly notion that we are a people connected to the landscape. After all, the nightly news is on the screen, not in the air.

In the twenty-first century we can't rely on something as antique and sentimental as a full moon.

Still, you've got to give that old mountain woman some credit. I mean, there will come a time when she can't get me on the phone. On some future day, I'll be out early, say, picking up the paper in the dark, and there it will be. A huge open letter from her to me. And I know I'll notice. I know I'll say, "I see you, old girl. Message received."

What We Remember

Her hair is wild from its contact with the pillow. Her conversation in cogent, but it stalls from time to time. There are blank spots. She knows where she was going with a story, but now the name of a cousin, or the year of the late snowstorm has disappeared, and she waits.

And yet, she can tell you exactly what she said to a mule on a summer day in 1943. "Your grandfather was away, working on the Norfolk and Western, and we were trying to get the hay in." The "we" includes my grandmother, my uncles and aunts and my mother, though the eldest of the children was only an early teenager.

"We had two men helping us and they were trying to make George pull a full-load of hay straight up the hill to the barn. Of course, he balked. So I climbed up on the wagon and took the reins.

"I said, 'Now George, get down and pull.' Then I let him go the way he wanted to go."

The mule, she remembers, spiraled around the hill, climbing gradually, making his way sensibly with such a heavy load. She draws a deep breath, rich, I'm sure, with the smell of cut timothy.

Michael Chitwood

Memory has its own logic. I cannot begin to tell you the date of my grandfather's funeral, but I can conjure a whiff of the green winter coat I wore to school that day. Its hood, always unzipped, lay flat aginast my shoulders. Inside, the fake fur was green, with one broad white horizontal stripe.

We record our memories in a private code. Just ask someone what they were doing when they heard about the assassination of JFK. You'll get an account of the math test they were taking, or the view from thewindow of a now long-junked sedan. That's how our memories serve us. They make it possible to return to the minute particulars of our lives.

On a recent visit to my mule-driving grandmother, I asked her about a story her sister-in-law had told to people who were compiling a history of the county. It concerned one of my grandfather's relatives.

"Oh, she got it all wrong," my grandmother huffed. "Her memory's bad, you know. He died in New Mexico, not Mexico, and he's not buried anywhere. His wife is totin' his ashes around in her pocketbook this very day."

I'll never forget the way her cane bounced on every syllable of "this very day."

Beans

When my father's and grandfather's jeans and overalls wore through at the knees or were stretched beyond use from too many tools being stuffed into them, my grandmother gave them a final washing and stacked them near her sewing machine. Once she had enough, she stitched a blanket from the still serviceable patches, the parts too good to throw away.

The Great Depression is a barely remembered blip in her childhood. You didn't miss what you'd never had, she once explained when I asked about those hard times. In the summer they ate from the garden and relished fish that came from Blackwater and Pigg rivers. In the winter, they ate what they'd canned, or salted, or smoked. She's fond of saying that the only parts of a pig that were wasted were the tail and the squeal. That's the way she always says it—"wasted." To her, anything that couldn't be made use of was a waste.

That includes every hour of daylight. In her hog and tobacco raising years, the days began when there was enough light to see by. Still, today when

Michael Chitwood

my phone rings before 8:30 A.M., I know it's either an emergency or she's calling just to say hello. She's been up for several hours.

A couple of mornings ago, just after eight, she called. "Y'all up?" she wanted to know. She sounded bright at first, but her tone soon took a downturn.

The last years have been hard. She broke her hip and can get around only with a walker. Arthritis has splayed the fingers of both hands to the point that she can barely hold a fork to eat. When I help her out of a car, or up steps, I can hear her bones popping and groaning.

Three sentences into our conversation she was crying. Poor old lady, you're probably thinking, she was in pain and feeling sorry for herself. She wanted a little sympathy.

Well, I'm sure she was in pain. She is constantly. But that wasn't why she was crying. She was crying because my father had picked a bushel of green beans in the cool of the early morning, and she couldn't help string them. Even if she couldn't walk, she sobbed, you'd think she could string some beans.

Of course, it wasn't the beans she was crying over. She saw that basket of beans heaped with her own mortality in the form of her uselessness. Nothing I could say could help her with that. We wear, fray, go threadbare. It can't be helped. It's actually a kind of luck to get to wear out, though that's hard to remember towards the end.

What I'm remembering now is that there are patches of time, remembered moments from another person's life, that never lose their usefulness. I'll save those, Grandma; they'll make a good blanket.

The Dance

I never saw him. I mean actually laid eyes on him. Of course, I've seen him hundreds of times in photographs and lately in the faces of my uncles as they age. But I never physically saw him.

His exit, and my entrance, were timed almost like a modern dance piece—him, representing old age and mortality, shuffling off stage-left, and me, representing youth and renewal, waiting stage-right to take his place. He died in March; I, his first grandchild, was born in April.

I always thought that explained why the whole family attributed my love of reading to him. The totem of my tribe is certainly not the bookmark. A socket wrench or shovel dozer maybe, but not a bookmark. My uncles, and sometimes even the aunts, would gently shake their heads when they would see me mesmerized by a book on a warm spring day. They'd sigh, half in explanation and half in excuse, saying, "Well, Daddy was always a reader."

It would have been nice, I often mused, to have a kindred spirit around. Maybe, he wouldn't have worn the same puzzled expression as the rest of the family when they looked at my college diploma. One of my uncles gave the words Summa Cum Laude the majority reading: "Some-a Come Loud, that's you all right."

I sometimes felt about as foreign with my family as that Latin phrase. When I heard about my cousin's wedding reception, I knew that my oddity would be proven for all to see. The youngest of the grandchildren, she was the first to take the stand that, no, she wasn't going to have the reception in the church fellowship hall like everybody else had done. She wanted a keg and a DJ so her friends could dance. Her mother reminded her that no one in our family would take the floor. If not the socket wrench or shovel dozer, then the totem for our crowd is certainly the folding chair, especially where music is concerned.

The music started and I was able to resist until the DJ put on "That Old Time Rock & Roll." Then it was revealed to all that one of the things I'd learned at college was that I loved to dance. I dragged my protesting wife onto the floor, and for that song we were the only ones dancing. After a few more songs and several other couples joining us, my grandmother motioned for me to come over to her chair.

I squatted beside her, ready for some advice about not making a spectacle of myself. "You know," she said, "Buren would walk all the way to Redwood if he heard there was going to be a string band and dancing. He just loved to dance."

At that moment, I knew exactly what the phrase blood kin meant. Though I'd never met, never even seen with infant eyes my maternal grandfather, I knew exactly how he felt down to his muscles. Whenever the music started, Granddaddy and I pulled somebody out onto the floor.

The Hunt Fund

When his gun went off, I jumped, bumping against the tree. Then the deer was crashing down the hill toward me. It sounded big as a cow. Just as it got to the creek bank twenty-five yards in front of me, it disappeared behind a tangle of honeysuckle vines and saplings. I had the gun raised, and the safety off. The deer would probably step out in a moment. From the blast of adrenaline my body had given itself, I started to shake.

"When did this get planned?" my wife asked as we dressed for work one morning, a week before season opened.

"Back in the summer," I answered.

My father and brother hunt the entire opening week of deer season. They go to the grocery store together to buy supplies and fill the back of Dad's Bronco with food, clothes, a Coleman stove, pots, plastic dishes and utensils. It's a family joke now that Dad stashes money away all year for the Hunt Fund, and he pays for everything during the week out of the fund.

I explained to my wife that I just wanted to get my share of the Hunt Fund. She pulled a towel from the closet and shut the bathroom door.

In late October and early November, whitetail deer become very active. They show up in odd places. The local paper will probably have a story about a terrified deer rampaging through a shopping mall parking lot or breaking its neck trying to leap a backyard privacy fence in a well-populated subdivision.

They aren't frightened by hunters. In most places, deer season doesn't open until the middle of November. The deer are in rut. The males will follow the females wherever they go. The males will also try to run other males away from their tract of woods. It makes for recklessness.

Because deer now have no natural predator other than man, the population, in many parts of the country, has outstripped the available territory. Deer have moved into the suburbs.

Any hunter who says he hunts to keep down the deer population, to maintain nature's balance, is a liar.

I grew up hunting, mostly rabbits. Every Saturday during rabbit season, from the time I was about twelve years old until I was about seventeen, my father and I would join Franklin Furrow, Dad's friend, and his son Rodney, my good friend, for a day of hunting. Many times other men and boys would come along.

Hitting Below the Bible Belt

My father and Franklin Furrow both had beagles. Most of the dogs were related. Our best jump dog was the daughter of Franklin's best jump dog. Sally and Dixie would sniff so hard inside a brushpile that they actually snorted. If there was a rabbit in there, he was coming out.

There were rules. You didn't shoot a rabbit on the jump. We wanted to hear the dogs run. You never shot in the direction of a person or dog. If the dogs jumped a deer, you didn't continue hunting until all the dogs came back. Rabbits run in a circle and won't go very far from where they are flushed. A deer will leave the voting district. Sometimes we had to stop the rabbit hunt, get in the truck and go find the dogs. We'd drive along back roads with the windows down. Two men and two boys packed in a truck cab, listening.

My brother was working his way down the hill from his stand, toward the creek. Either his shot had hit the deer and it had died behind the honeysuckle, or it would flush very shortly.

I walked toward the tangle with my rifle up. The deer broke away from us, heading up the creek. Picking them up and putting them down, as my father says.

How can you be so surprised when fully prepared? I swung and fired. I don't know where the first shot hit. I know it wasn't the deer. The second shot hit a pine tree square in the middle. The deer disappeared into the woods.

My brother and I walked to the tangle of honeysuckle the deer had hid behind. The leaves were splattered with bright blood. It was crimson, almost unnaturally red.

"Damn it, damn it, damn it," my brother said, taking off his cap. "I *thought* I hit that deer. Damn it." He walked up the creek a little way, then walked back. He looked in the direction the deer had gone as though he might be able to see it. "Damn it," he said. "I hate that."

I work in an office in the Research Triangle Park, North Carolina. My wife works in an office there. About 34,000 people come to work each day in the Park. It's one of the largest concentrations of Ph.Ds and engineers in the United States. We all work in offices or laboratories—eight, ten, twelve hours inside each day. When we have finished working, most of us drive home and go inside our houses. Maybe we go to the mall, or catch a movie.

More than likely, you're inside right now. When was the last time you were seriously cold? Which direction was the wind blowing today? Was it cloudy when the sun came up this morning? If you stood in your yard, would it be quiet enough to hear a leaf striking bare branches on its way to the ground?

The company I work for has just purchased equipment for research in virtual reality. The engineers tell me that eventually you will be able to drive through a town, walk through a house or rearrange the furniture in a room without moving from in front of the computer monitor. You can even have virtual sex, and it's much safer than the real thing.

Our best jump dog was an escape artist. She was a master hunter and hated the confinement of the dog lot. I would watch from my sister's bedroom to discover the latest escape route. Sometimes she found a soft spot and tunneled under the fence. Other times it was over the top, climbing by hooking her fore paws over the wire and pushing with her hind legs.

After she was almost hit on the highway during one of her breakouts, Dad rigged a leash to slide on a wire inside the lot. It gave her run of the place and still kept her safe.

It was my job to feed the dogs each day after school, a chore I did with varying degrees of promptness. Sally's body was stiff when I found it dangling halfway down the outside of the fence. She must have come over sometime that morning. I cradled her cold rigid body to free one hand to unsnap the leash, her noose. Her awkward stiffness and my tears made it a difficult task.

"We'll have to track it," my brother says, still pacing up and down the creek bank. He has been spanking his leg with his cap. Now he puts it back on and starts off in the direction the deer went. He's crouched, scanning the leaves.

"Here," he points to a few splotches of blood. "You stand here," he says. He moves ahead. "Okay, here's some more," he says, pointing to where he wants me to stand. I wait while he scouts the forest floor. If he doesn't see anything after twenty yards or so, he comes back to me and heads in a different direction.

Dawn in the woods is slow motion. The light soaks

in like a drizzle. The landscape forms out of the darkness like the images on a Polaroid. Christmas morning, and there, materializing, is the happy boy with his new shotgun.

The squirrel was working a pine cone. My father whispered in my ear, so close his Saturday stubble scraped my face.

"Take a deep breath and squeeze the trigger; don't jerk it."

He braced me with his chest at my back, his arms around me in a light hug. All during church the next day, I touched my shoulder, proud of the tenderness.

Our stands are homemade. I had helped my father and brother set them up a week before the season opened. "This is a good place," my brother said as he tightened the chain that held the stand to the tree. "I got that big one here two years ago."

The stand is a ladder with a small platform on top. The platform has a semi-circle cut into it, which fits around the trunk of a tree. You find a tree the correct size and lash the stand to it. It's best to choose a smooth tree because it will be your back rest.

You should get to your stand before daylight. You climb up, keeping your rifle pointed away from you. You turn carefully and sit down. Your feet rest on the topmost rung. Settle in, you're going to be here awhile.

Still-hunting is our native Zen. You must remain as quiet as possible. You must be absolutely alert. You can scan about two-hundred degrees of the circle of surrounding landscape without straining unduly. You must listen into the other one-hundred sixty degrees.

I stopped hunting during my college years. I was the first member of my family, my extended family including grandparents, aunts, uncles and cousins, to attend a residential college, which meant I was away during most of hunting season. Also, thanks to some courses I had taken, I had questions about hunting. Mostly, though, it was just because I was away.

My brother did not go to college. His hunting experience is seamless. My education, which my parents paid for, allowed me to get a good job, inside, at a desk far from my home county.

My brother is a heavy equipment operator, by all accounts one of the best in the county. He lives four miles from my parents on land purchased with money my parents gave him, the equivalent of the sum required for my college education. Which is more real, an idea or an acre?

The week before season opened, a deer was killed at the mouth of our exit onto Interstate 40. It must have been hit by an eighteen-wheeler because it was reduced to fairly small pieces that were scattered along the highway, on the shoulder and in the middle of the road.

All week long, the commuters, speaking into cellular phones, sipping their coffee from wide-bottomed mugs, catching up on the world with National Public Radio, rendered the chunks of meat into a long, red stain.

• • •

There was a scooped-out place in the leaves and a large splash of blood at the center of it. "He lay down for a while," my brother said. We tracked the blood trail for about a mile. "It shouldn't be much farther," my brother said.

Three-hundred yards more and we saw the deer standing in the woods. Some of his intestines were dangling in the leaves. My brother dropped to one knee and brought the cross-hairs of his scope to bear. The deer fell with his shot. When we got to the deer we discovered that the first shot had broken his right hind leg.

"I'm glad we found you," my brother said to the deer as he pulled intestines and lungs from the chest cavity. He was field dressing the animal so the meat would be in the best shape possible. He was up to his elbows inside the deer. "I would have felt terrible if we hadn't found you."

When the breeze stirs, the stand sways with the tree. You sway with the stand and the tree. It's a gentle dance because the roots have a solid hold.

My father had a business meeting he couldn't skip on the second morning of deer season, but he came home at noon to see if we had any luck. We had my brother's deer in the back of his pickup.

We told my father the story of the creek and the tracking. My brother and I told it in tandem, each breaking in to add details or mention landmarks we knew our father would know.

"I hate it, but I've got to go back to work," Dad

said after we'd finished. He handed me a twenty-dollar bill.

"Y'all get some lunch. This week everything's on the Hunt Fund."

We've thrown a chain across the biggest limb of the maple at the side of the house to hold the buck while we skin it.

"You'll have to lift him up until I can get the chain hooked," my brother says. I hook my hands under the buck's front legs in a kind of hug and strain to lift him.

"A little higher."

I have to get a better grip. I pull the deer to me, brace him against my chest. My face is buried in the brown, black and grey of his shoulder. It's all I can do to get him high enough.

Old Songs

We all piled into the back of someone's pickup. An accident would have taken out an entire generation of the youth of Redwood Methodist Church, but we weren't going to have an accident. What harm could possibly come to young people on their way to sing Christmas carols to old folks?

I have to admit that I didn't actually care for the singing part. I mean, I liked the songs, particularly "Go Tell It On the Mountain," which always sounded to me like it could have been written by someone from our community. What made me uncomfortable was watching those wrinkled faces as we sang. In some the eyes would spark with the memory of the tunes. Others stared and seemed to be confused by the mass of young people standing before them. Were these their grandchildren, they seemed to be wondering? Why were there so many of them? What were their names?

We would head to town and do the old folks home first, and then drive down the back roads near the church and unload in yards to sing for the elderly who didn't get out much anymore. These were old women mostly, their husbands ten or twenty years dead. The women would hobble to their doors and stand while we ran through two numbers. Then they would want to kiss everybody, and we would form a reluctant line to receive a lilac-scented smooch.

What I really enjoyed about the caroling was the ride between visitations. The chill air whipping through the back of the truck gave us a little-needed excuse to pack tightly, boy, girl, boy, girl. I was a master at scrambling back into the pickup bed so that I landed between the two girls I was most interested in. If the moon was clouded over and we were on a particularly dark stretch of road, there might be a little kissing of a less hesitant sort.

This particular evening I wasn't paying any attention to where the driver was taking us. We made several of the usual stops at houses beginning to look a bit ramshackled. And then we were pulling into a familiar yard, my grandmother's. I looked around to see if shock was registering on everyone, but the other kids were happily leaping over the sides of the bed. Though our first time here, this seemed natural to everyone.

And there she was, like all the others, bracing herself on the door knob, smiling at the song, motioning for us to come by for a kiss. This is a mistake, I almost said aloud. She's not...not....

Everyone was heading for the truck, but I was frozen in the seared grass of the yard. The other kids called to me. I waved them on. I was near my house, so they thought they understood. The truck revved and was gone while I watched through the window as the frail old lady made her way back to the TV. Then I walked the dark path to my house alone.

The Harvest

For the past five decades, Curtis, my father-in-law, has spent the first several weeks of Fall harvesting his farm's huge corn crop. The corn is the major source of food for the farm's large dairy herd. For Curtis, cutting the corn is the culmination of the year's work. It's the harvest that will either see the farm through another year or, if the crop is lean, have him scrambling to find feed for the cows.

Several times I've ridden in the cab of the massive tractor with him as he spirals toward the center of a field, pulling the harvesting machine. My mind always wanders as we make our noisy crawl along the rows, but Curtis seems to examine every stalk before it enters the cutter. The pace is glacial to me, like an hour hand making it's slow turn around the face of a giant clock. But Curtis' attention never flags. It's as if he's studying the very dust for its lessons and memorizing each round of corn as it's cut.

Late in August, Curtis entered the hospital for by-pass surgery, and when it came time to cut the corn the scar down the middle of his chest was freshly pink. He had to watch from the house as his son and a nephew made the rounds in the fields.

On a Saturday in the middle of the harvest, he and I were discussing the progress of the work. He watched as the truck bringing corn dragged a dust cloud toward the silos and suddenly said, "This is the first time in forty-nine years that I haven't cut the corn." Amazing as that plain statement is, I can't imagine doing anything every year for forty-nine years, I was more amazed by the tone with which this seventy-eight-year-old man delivered it. No self-pity. No anger. Not even relief. He said it as though it was an idea he was trying out, speaking it aloud just to see how it sounded.

His tanned face gave no clues as to what he was feeling, which made me all the more hungry to know. What did this mean to him?

I made some comment about that being a long time, hoping to draw him out, get him to explain himself a little more. He sat quietly, watching the truck disappear back into the field. Then he said brightly, "I heard a good joke the other day. This city fellow stopped at a country gas station and was filling his car when a local guy pulled up in his pickup and started pumping gas too. The city dude took a deep breath, looked around and said, 'This place is so clean and beautiful. It must be a healthy place to live. What's the mortality rate around here?' The local farmer looked over the hood of his truck, smiled and said, 'One to one.'"

Curtis repeated the "One to one" with a warm chuckle. And after forty-nine years that was all the explaining he was going to do.

Getting the Story Straight

Here's the story as I heard it.

One day, after everybody had something to eat and left for school and work, Grandma went to the shed, got out an ax and headed for the little hill just in back of the house. The hill was covered with a stand of pines that Granddaddy had been meaning to cut. Grandma went to work, sometimes spending the whole day there, the tattoo of her chopping echoing at the house like the muffled beating of a heart.

She worked two, maybe it was three months, until she'd felled every pine on that hill.

The story was told throughout my adolescence by my mother, my aunts and uncles, other relatives. Sometimes it would include the phrase "that Mary, she could work like a man." I took it as a parable of her strength, her near-pioneer pluck. It was told to me, I thought, to teach diligence, over-the-top effort and to let me know that spit-in-your-eye determination was part of my genetic programming.

Then one Thanksgiving, an aunt was tuning up for the usual recitation of the story, but she started it with, "V.B. had just shipped out for Korea and

Momma went to the shed and got the ax."

Wait a minute. Had that always been there, the part about uncle V.B.? He was the first-born, witty and reckless, a constant source of one or another form of entertainment. His antics often landed him in trouble, which somehow made him even more lovable. Had this always been part of the story—a part I just hadn't attached any importance to?

Like a slight twist on a kaleidoscope, this small addition changed everything. What was once a meaningless detail was now the key to the story. This wasn't a tale of perseverance. This was the story of a woman handling an emotional thunderclap in a place and time that had never heard of counselors or therapy groups.

Our narratives are timeless because we're not and our perspective shifts. *Romeo and Juliet*, for instance, has become less a tale of young love for me and more a caution about clannish pride and inflexibility.

The new story of my grandmother literally pining away has deepened. It's taken on the complex hues of psychological coloring. But, I also realize, it remains a story of strength, a strength of a much tougher sort. With pride, I still imagine the slap of the ax and its echo against the clapboard homeplace, the sound from those scrub pines like a wild heart beating.

The Gesture

It's a mere flick of a gesture. The driver's index finger jumping up from the steering wheel and then quickly tucking back down. You need to be paying attention to even see it.

And you don't see it much around town. You have to get out in the country where it's the standard greeting for every car passing. It's the quick physical equivalent of "How ya doing?"

It's a gesture I hadn't seen in quite a while, but when the white-haired gent in the pickup gave me the sign the other day, it was as though his index finger had pulled a trigger and a whole nearly forgotten memory went off in my head.

My grandfather lifted his finger from the wheel, nodded his head slightly and started to chuckle. The smoke of his Lucky Strike made his words and even his laughter into ghosts that wafted in the air all around me.

"That fella we just passed, well, he and I decided to go down to the river one Saturday night for some fishing. He was always complaining about being broke and said he didn't even have the money to buy a fishing license but I told him not to worry about it.

"Well, we had no more than got our lines wet when this voice comes out of the dark above us on the bank. 'I'll need to see some papers, gentlemen,' the game warden says.

"I dropped my pole and tore off right through the river and that warden came in behind me. We hit the other bank at full gallop and cut a swath through Ned Hudson's cane field. I ran until I was almost to the state road. Then I let the warden catch up. He grabs my shirt and says, 'Alright, you.' But I just start rubbing my leg and say, 'Warden, you know how it is when one of those cramps hit you, don't you? I just have to run to work them out and that one that hit me back there on the river bank just then was a powerful one.'

"Then I pull out my wallet and show him my license, everything nice and legal. He stomps off toward his car and my buddy was halfway back to his house by then with a nice mud cat and no license whatsoever."

Here the old man fights both laughter and smoke for his breath. He pounds the steering wheel with the heel of his hand and says, "Ah God, I'll never forget it."

It was just a slight gesture. A small human movement on a country road from a white-haired driver going way too slow. But from that quick greeting, I heard again the rich, warm, ghostly laughter and, Ah God, I'll never forget it.

Thanksgiving

Thanksgiving has given us some of our most over-cooked, sticky, soppy mush, and, no, I'm not talking about Aunt Tootsie's sweet potato casserole. I'm talking about the cards, commercials and TV shows that try to recapture for us the over-the-river-and-through-the-woods warm family feeling of this holiday.

Now, don't get me wrong, Thanksgiving is my favorite holiday. But I hold the turkey massacre in high regard for reasons that would make Norman Rockwell nauseous.

Here's the scene. It's Thanksgiving Day 1970. Our tribe, which consists of my mother's brothers and sisters, their spouses and children, has gathered at the ancestral home. The hubbub from the three dozen or so people has stilled while my father asks the blessing. I'm at the head of a line of children, clutching a plate to my chest, waiting for this long prayer to be over. You can see me only because I'm first in line. That year, I was the shortest kid in the seventh grade. I had been the shortest kid in the sixth grade, and from all indications I would be the shortest kid in the eighth grade. I looked up to other boys; girls towered over me. I was fiercely, and privately, embarrassed about this.

The prayer ends, and before the buzz of conversation picks back up, Uncle Flukie, lovable old Uncle Flukie, shouts a question across the room to me.

"Hey, Michael, how's your lawsuit going?"

Now, I should have known to start loading my plate and only open my mouth when I was ready to put some dressing in it. Uncle Flukie is famous for his earthy insights and scatological pearls of wisdom. If you offered up a wishful thought around him, he would respond with, "Yeah, and people in Hell want ice water."

So, I should have just reached for the brown-and-serve roll and kept silent. But, noooooo.

"What lawsuit?" the miniature twelve-year-old said. The room was still.

"I heard you were suing the town of Rocky Mount for building the sidewalks too close to your behind." The room erupted.

Uncle Flukie had made me the straight man and butt (excuse the pun) of the joke. But don't judge him too harshly. Like all master comics, his timing was perfect. The *secret* that I was painfully aware of my lack of height was out, but it wasn't revealed to a pack of strangers. Before I sat down, I got hugs from my mother and two aunts, and grandma made sure I got two desserts. The youngest uncle called every other pass play to me after lunch. And when no one was looking, Flukie gave me a wink. It said, "See that wasn't so bad. You'll live through it."

Grandma's Teeth

My grandmother keeps her teeth in the cupboard. Chalk white and embedded in unnaturally pink gums, they're not in much danger of receiving any lasting stain or getting worn down because she rarely uses them. At least, she rarely uses them for eating, but I'll get to that in a minute.

I don't remember a time when she had her own teeth. I'm sure she had them when I was young, but I don't recall broad smiles. When I think of her laughing, it's with her head thrown back, eyes closed and gums gleaming.

She claims her "store-bought" teeth hurt her, so she only wears them to the most formal occasions— weddings, christenings, funerals. My mother tries to explain to her that she's never worn them enough to get used to them and that they probably would stop hurting after awhile. But grandma sees no need to go through the discomfort.

During the 1940s, with my grandfather working for the railroad and away for long stretches, she kept the small family farm going, along the way having seven children and raising six of them to adulthood.

She was too busy to have much truck with appearances, and she's carried that attitude into old age.

Besides, Grandma discovered another use for her teeth, one she relishes much more than mere eating. Grandma uses her teeth as a test.

With adults, it's a mild little check of the nerves. "I can't get up," she'll say to an unknowing visitor, "but the tea glasses are in the cupboard there. You help yourself." Then she watches like a cat, waiting for the sharp intake of breath.

But with children it's a different story. She'll hobble into the kitchen to dole out a snack and while the child is munching away she'll say, "I've got something I want to show you."

Then she'll plop the teeth on the table and search the little face for the emotions passing there. Some kids bolt. Some are immediately fascinated and pick up the teeth. Mostly it's the great -grandkids that get the teeth test; I think she knows anyone else might think it way out of line.

So what's she up to? I know she'd never explain, but I think I've figured it out. If a child recoils, her reaction is immediate. She puts the teeth back in the cupboard. If the child is intrigued, she leaves her choppers out awhile. Kids can even play with them if they want.

Whether the child sees a threatening grimace or toothy smile, eventually the teeth go back into the cupboard. Her life, she'll tell you, was "Root pig or die," and her message to her brood is this: fun is transitory, but so is fear. No matter what falls in front of you it won't last forever. Your job, child, is to keep going, teeth or no teeth.

Appalachian Anvils

When the talk turns to Southern femininity, the phrase "Southern Belle" gets dusted off and passed around as if everyone knew what it was, or is, or has been. Anyway, I have to say that growing up in the southern regions of the Blue Ridge Mountains the only bells I ever heard about were in the steeple of the Methodist Church.

So, lest non-natives think that *ALL* females born and raised in the lower right-hand section of the country are something called belles, who worry about the cotillion and bat their eyes fetchingly at gentlemen, I feel bound to explain another sort of Southern woman.

Let me give you an example. When my grandmother was in her early seventies, she began to have some trouble getting around. At first, it was just a matter of using the kitchen table and then the edge of the counter and chair arms and backs to make her way through the house. Then she had to get one of those canes that have the three-pronged rubber-tipped bottoms. But despite the difficulty she still managed to cook the meals for herself and one of my uncles. She took a daily quarter-mile walk to the mailbox. She checked on the tomatoes.

She even took up with a cat. Well, actually a cat took up with her, but when the stray started coming around the house she began to feed it. This was stunning to all of us, as she never had much use for pets. Mules, cows, pigs—useful, working animals, or animals to be eaten, yes,—but troublesome creatures like cats and house dogs, no.

But we thought maybe she was lonely and were glad the cat had found her. She never named it though. Just called it "Cat." Or "That animal." But she did feed it, even actually cooked it some chicken once. And, of course, the cat took to this treatment. It grew affectionate and started following Grandma to the mailbox, rubbing against her legs as she walked, darting between her steps.

Thinking back on it now we should have seen it coming, but I was floored when I arrived at Grandma's after she summoned me one Saturday afternoon. The cat lay beside its food bowl, graveyard dead. Grandma's .22 rifle was on the kitchen table.

"Oh God, Grandma. You shot it."

"I did."

"But why?"

"I'll have no trouble out of a cat. It nearly tripped me today, and I can't take a broken hip."

"But while it was eating?"

"And I had to feed it. I've gotten a little shaky in my old age. I didn't want to miss. You know once you feed a cat, you can't get rid of it. It's like a man that way. Now bury that thing and come inside; I've got a warm chocolate pie."

I did precisely as I was told. See, you don't ar-

Michael Chitwood

gue with this type of Southern woman. Southern Belle? Call them Appalachian Anvils. And they will suffer no trouble out of men or cats.

The Use of It

"Oh, he didn't give it to me, but he said I could have the use of it." With those words my mountain relatives might explain how it is that they are using someone else's chainsaw, or tiller, or extension ladder. It's an expression that gives full due to the value tools have in what is still a largely agrarian lifestyle. Tools make life easier, and the right tool can make even a difficult task if not a joy then at least bearable.

It's a phrase I've been repeating to myself silently the last week or so, because I've come to know just how accurate it is. The tool, in this case, is a poem by Robert Morgan, a poet originally from the North Carolina mountains, and the use of his words over the last dozen days has helped me greatly.

About two weeks ago, I was visiting my parents when, around 9:30 one evening, the phone rang. My bachelor uncle, who still lives in the family home, was calling for my mother's help. My grandmother had fallen. We quickly got on shoes and coats and made the short drive to Grandma's. We found her in a heap, an aunt holding her hands. Her left foot was turned at a sickeningly odd angle to her leg and a pool of blood stained the carpet beneath the ankle. The ambulance had already been called.

Grandma, who is eighty-seven, has been barely able to walk for the last couple years. But she'd managed to stay in the old house and negotiate the numerous steps and turns which years of additions had made to the once log structure. As I looked at her on the floor, helplessly waiting for the rescue squad to arrive, I knew a hard change was coming.

My mother and aunt rushed out the door ahead of Grandma's stretcher to go with her to the hospital, and alone I watched the men load her into the rescue unit. The double doors thudded in my chest as they were closed.

And then I heard lines from Morgan's "When the Ambulance Came" almost as if someone in the room had spoken them. I was suddenly in the poem with Morgan. "When the ambulance came for Grandma/ ...I watched them lift the stretcher/ through the kitchen door./ One attendant stood in mud by/ the steps where we threw the/ dishwater and leftovers for the chickens:/ I saw a piece of cabbage stick on his shoe." I almost said the heartbreaking last lines aloud. "...[H]ow the driver cursed the torn/ roads over the mountain/ when he slammed the spattered door/ on her seventy years/ of staying home."

It wasn't an easy comfort. But it was as though a respected uncle had stepped to my side and said, "Hurts like Hell, don't it?" Together we watched the red lights fade and for that companionship, for that forlorn but shared farewell, I was grateful.

This One

"Well, how's my girl this morning?"

No answer.

"I saw your boyfriend in the dining room this morning. He was asking about you."

Here the young woman in the white dress, white shoes and latex gloves turns to the visitor and says, "This one looks at you like she'd like to get her hands around your throat."

The visitor says nothing. What do you say to a young woman, the closest one to a "girl" in the room, who is trying to do her job. And such a job it is. The place is called a Health Care Center, but there's precious little health here. What is here is the smell of urine and regurgitated saltless meals.

It's probably the young woman's first job, and it's full of hopelessness. These people never get better. Many of these people can not remember their own names. They foul the sheets regularly. Though it's a clean place and well run, the antiseptic can't keep up. It's the best such place in town. The young woman is trying to be kind and trying to keep her mind occupied so that she doesn't think of the task at hand or how "this one" is looking at her.

This one, the visitor thinks, is eighty-seven years old.

This one has no boyfriend and hasn't had the loving touch of a spouse since 1958. Thirty-nine years and she did not even consider another man.

This one had seven children and raised six of them.

This one cleared two acres of pine trees, by herself with an ax, while raising those six children and two crops of tobacco.

This one could drive a team of mules as well as any man. And did often.

This one, this one here, when her legs failed her and she could no longer work outside made dresses, shirts, skirts, ties, jackets and entire men's suits, with vests, to outfit her daughters and sons, their husbands and wives and eleven grandchildren.

This one would use a hoe as a cane until she could get to the snake beside the woodpile. Then she'd risk a fall to chop off that spade head.

This one looks at you that way because she lived fiercely. This one's fierce God, if He is not cruel, will come for her soon.

Opening the Grave

I'm sure there's some scrap of linguistic history that explains the curious phrase I'd just heard, and I'm sure I'd heard it used before, but the phrase had never sounded as odd, or as right, to me before. I'd never wondered at it before.

My mother, running through the list of services covered by the fee you paid the funeral home, said, "And, of course, that includes opening the grave."

Opening the grave? As if it had been there all along, a room to be unlocked and, of course, entered.

And, in this case, it had been there all along—for my entire life. My grandfather had died the February before I was born in April. Since the church's cemetery was just across the state road from our house, I grew up first playing around and then helping to mow between the tombstones. All those years, it was right there under the big stone marked "Hall." On the left, was my grandfather's name with his two dates and, on the right, my grandmother's with just one date. It was always there and I didn't think about the day when the stone would be numerically balanced.

Michael Chitwood

"Was it unexpected?" acquaintances asked as they shook our hands in the flower-filled room. "Yes," we said, "she had been in the nursing home, but over the last month or so seemed to be improving, getting a little stronger." It was true and when you'd visit she'd talk about when she might go home.

In fact, she'd improved so much that it was decided that she could visit with the whole family at my aunt's house on Mother's Day. It would do her good.

It was a harrowing day. Grandma was helpless, frightened by the awkwardness of being lifted from cars and soon grew tired of sitting up. "It was pitiful," my uncle told me. "Mama was terrified and I was too." When the nurses asked her later if she had a good time she said, "Well, I was uncomfortable, and I could see my house, the house I've lived in for sixty-seven years." I heard my mother tell that part of the story to dozens of people at the funeral home.

On Mother's Day, Grandma had realized she wasn't going back to that house, the house in which she'd given birth to and raised her children, the house that had for thirty-nine years been the hub for the wheeling lives of eleven grandchildren.

Unexpected? She, like everyone else, now knew those familiar doors were locked to her. She was also well known for making things happen her way. There was no onslaught of pneumonia, no sudden heart attack, but unexpected? It took her just one week to open the only door she could now get to and with her usual no nonsense manner, she entered.